Evil

Also available in this series:
Creation
War and Peace

Forthcoming:
God in Action
Science and Religion

Problems in Theology

Evil
A Reader

Edited by
Jeff Astley, David Brown and Ann Loades

T & T CLARK
A Continuum imprint
LONDON • NEW YORK

T&T CLARK LTD
A Continuum imprint

The Tower Building   15 East 26th Street
11 York Road   New York, NY 10010
London SE1 7NX, UK   USA

www.continuumbooks.com

Copyright © T&T Clark Ltd, 2003

All rights reserved. No part of this publication may be reproduced or transmitted in any form or by any means, electronic or mechanical, including photocopy, recording or any information retrieval system, without permission in writing from the publishers or their appointed agents.

Every effort has been made to contact the copyright holders of material featured in this book. The publisher welcomes any queries from those copyright holders we may have been unable to contact.

British Library Cataloguing-in-Publication Data
A catalogue record for this book is available from the British Library

ISBN 0 567 08975 4 (paperback)
ISBN 0 567 08976 2 (hardback)

Typeset by RefineCatch Limited, Bungay, Suffolk
Printed and bound in Great Britain by MPG Books Ltd, Bodmin, Cornwall

Contents

Preface   vii

Introduction: Reading the readings   1

1 – Evil, protest and response   5
1.1 Outrage and rebellion; 1.2 Theodicy and bad faith; 1.3 Finding God in evil; 1.4 Protest atheism and the cross; 1.5 Suffering and the death of Christ; 1.6 Survival, endurance and the Holocaust; Topics for discussion

2 – The Buddha and Kierkegaard on suffering: Two religions compared   30
2.1 The Buddha, suffering and enlightenment; 2.2 On not explaining; 2.3 On direct experience; 2.4 Nirvana; 2.5 Compassion and sacrifice; 2.6 Self and suffering; 2.7 Kierkegaard on truth, Job and Christ; 2.8 Some explanatory notes on Buddhism; Topics for discussion

3 – The varieties of theodicy   56
3.1 The problem posed; 3.2 Some solutions offered; 3.3 The principle of plenitude and the screening of God; 3.4 Evil as non-being; 3.5 The free will defence; 3.6 The vale of soul-making; Topics for discussion

4 – The logic of theodicy   79
4.1 The best possible world? 4.2 Maximizing satisfaction? 4.3 Necessary evil?; 4.4 The cost-effectiveness of evil and the quantifying of pain; Topics for discussion

Acknowledgements   101
Further reading   103
Index of subjects   109
Index of names   111

Preface

Courses in theology and religious studies in universities, colleges and sixth forms are increasingly 'topic-based' or 'problem-based', and usually form part of modular programmes of study for first degrees or AS/A2 level qualifications. Teachers and students often find it difficult to access relevant primary material for the different topics that they have selected to study. Many textbooks are too general to be of more than limited value, and the same is true of selections of readings.

This series of readers in *Problems in Theology* is designed to meet this need by focusing on particular controversial themes and issues. Each volume provides a set of carefully selected readings from primary sources, together with a brief introductory essay, topics for discussion or further study, and a select bibliography. A particular advantage of the format adopted here is that teachers and students can use the material selectively, constructing their own educational pathway through the problem.

The readings chosen for these books have been tested out with undergraduate classes in the University of Durham. Much of this material will also be accessible, however, to sixth form students of religious studies, as well as to those studying theology on ordination courses and in adult education classes.

The editors wish to thank all who have assisted in this project by helping in the selection, referencing and trial-testing of material, by copy-typing and editing the text, or by securing permissions. Particular thanks go to Paul Fletcher, Greta Gleeson, Evelyn Jackson, Declan O'Sullivan and Isabel Wollaston; and to David Webster for writing 'Some Explanatory Notes on Buddhism'.

Notes on the text

The passages are printed (except for omissions, indicated by three or four full stops) as in the original text, with the same spelling, punctuation etc. In most cases, however, notes within the readings have been omitted.

From time to time the editors have added their own explanatory comments. These are printed in italics and enclosed in square brackets.

Introduction
Reading the readings

The problem of evil is perhaps the most serious challenge to belief in an all-loving, creator God. In this anthology we explore both the practical, existential or spiritual problem of coping with evil, and the more theoretical, intellectual or theological problem of explaining it. As the first two chapters of readings indicate, these two approaches cannot readily be separated in human experience and reflection, including the experience and reflection of lived religion. Strictly speaking, however, *theodicy* focuses on the second, explanatory, task. It is the attempt to justify the justice and goodness of God in the face of the evidence for the prosecution that is provided by the pain and suffering caused by events of Nature ('natural evil' or 'physical evil') and by the actions of free agents ('moral evil').

As George Pattison insists, the proper response to evil – even in a religious context – is outrage (see Reading 1.1). The classic illustration of this is Ivan Karamazov's challenge, from Dostoyevsky's famous novel. Many modern theologians agree that 'a theodicy is not worth reading if it does not allow the screams of our society to be heard' (Surin, 1.2). Christian theology is often encouraged, therefore, to protest against any portrayal of God's relation to evil other than that provided by the 'voice within' heard by Elie Wiesel in the death camp: that God was there too, hanging on this gallows (1.3); 'any other answer would be blasphemy' (Moltmann, 1.4). For Christians, this is potent imagery. In Christian theology Christ's suffering must always be key to any attempt either to explain evil or to cope with it (1.5).[1] For Jews, however, it is the 'Shoah' or 'Holocaust' of six million innocents by the Nazis that represents

---

[1] See also Donald M. MacKinnon, *Borderlands of Theology*, London, Lutterworth, 1968, pp. 90–6; Diogenes Allen, 'Natural Evil and the Love of God', in M. M. Adams and R. M. Adams (eds), *The Problem of Evil*, Oxford, Oxford University Press, 1990, pp. 189–208.

their main stumbling block – and catalyst – for theodicy (see 1.6 and Eckardt, 1.4).

With the readings in Chapter 2, we move to the Buddhist tradition for an alternative perspective on suffering and a different analysis of the ways to cope with and explain it (for background information, see 2.8, Some explanatory notes on Buddhism). Early Buddhism is concerned primarily with the practical task of overcoming the universal fact of the suffering, misery or 'unsatisfactoriness' of existence, which is understood as closely tied to the human instinct to crave for and cling to experience and life, and seeks to show how to escape such a negative feature of our condition (2.1, 2.3). Unlike some other species of theodicy, a great deal is left unexplained in Buddhism; even questions about the gods are 'not profitable' for its essentially practical purpose (2.2). This feature of Buddhism's distinctive approach to the problem of evil needs to be borne in mind when studying Buddhist views on *nirvana*, compassion and self-sacrifice (2.4, 2.5).

At the conclusion of this chapter of readings we return to a Judaeo-Christian perspective and 'the salvific potential of suffering' (Mellor, 2.6). The readings show how this is expressed in the struggle of Job before God,[2] and (supremely for the Christian) in the Way of Christ – a Way that allows the burden of suffering to remain the same and 'yet . . . become light' (Kierkegaard, 2.7).

With the readings in Chapters 3 and 4, we move more firmly into the debates that perceive evil as a theological problem for theism (belief in God) that demands a theological explanation. In its most blunt formulation the problem states that either God cannot or God will not abolish the world's evil. If God cannot, then God is surely not all-powerful ('omnipotent' – that is, capable of doing anything that can be done); if God will not, then God is surely not morally perfect. Thus presented, the problem of evil 'is essentially a logical problem' (Mackie, 3.1), for it appears to be inconsistent to believe *both* that the world is created by a wholly good God who is omnipotent and omniscient[3] *and* that evil exists (Penelhum, 3.1).

---

[2] On the Book of Job, see 1.1 and also Samuel Terrien, *Job: Poet of Existence*, New York, Bobbs-Merrill, 1957; Nahum N. Glatzer (ed.), *The Dimensions of Job*, New York, Schocken Books, 1969; Brian Horne, *Imagining Evil*, London, Darton, Longman & Todd, 1996, Ch. 2; David Brown, *Discipleship and Imagination: Christian Tradition and Truth*, Oxford, Oxford University Press, 2000, Ch. 4.

[3] That is, capable of knowing everything that can be known. For introductory discussions of omnipotence and omniscience as attributes of God, see Brian Davies, *Thinking about God*, London, Chapman, 1985, Ch. 7; Peter Vardy, *The Puzzle of God*, London, Collins, 1990, Chs 12 and 13.

Within the Christian tradition a variety of attempts have been made to resolve this apparent contradiction. These different 'solutions' are sometimes represented as forming part of one of two families of explanation, which have become labelled the Augustinian and the Irenaean (3.2).[4] Within these families, a home may be found for such disparate responses to the problem of evil as the 'principle of plenitude' (3.3), 'evil as non-being' (3.4), the 'free will defence' – a defence that has been applied both to our individual sins and to humankind's 'original sin' (3.5),[5] and the 'vale of soul-making theodicy' (3.6).

Chapter 4 collects together readings that discuss a number of more philosophical issues in theodicy, all of which share a common theme. These issues include the claim that this is the best possible world, despite its evils,[6] perhaps because it contains second-order goods such as sympathy and courage that could only exist 'on the back', as it were, of first-order suffering. The chapter also samples the debate as to whether God *is* obliged to create the best possible world (4.1), the question as to whether maximising happiness is a coherent goal, even for God (4.2), the contention of Richard Swinburne and others that natural evils must exist in order for humans to have knowledge of how to create or prevent evil (4.3), and arguments about the 'cost-effectiveness of evil' and the acceptability of the practice within theodicy of quantifying suffering (4.4). This last arena of discussion illustrates how profound and deeply felt religious and moral attitudes underlie even the most abstract analyses within theodicy.

---

[4] After St Augustine of Hippo (AD 354–430) and St Irenaeus (AD 130–200), respectively.

[5] Traditionally the free will defence has also been applied to supernatural agents of evil that are thought of as having rebelled against God (see Peter Vardy, *The Puzzle of Evil*, London, HarperCollins, 1992, Ch. 10).

[6] For an account of the classical statement of this view in the eighteenth-century 'optimism' of Leibniz and others, see John Hick, *Evil and the God of Love*, London, Macmillan, 1966, Ch. VII. For a famous response in a very different genre, see Voltaire's *Candide* (1758, many editions and translations).

1 Evil, protest and response

1.1 Outrage and rebellion

George Pattison, *A Short Course in the Philosophy of Religion*, London, SCM, 2001, pp. 162, 164–7, 169, 172

Voltaire wrote graphically of the horrors of war and of the other evils that human beings perpetrate upon each other, yet at the same time his reflections on the question of evil seem finally to come to rest on the problem of natural evil as manifested by the Lisbon earthquake. It is indeed characteristic of the distance separating the early modern approach to the question from our own that whereas the earthquake served not only Voltaire but eighteenth-century Europe as a whole as a paradigm of evil, a test case for theodicy, *our* question centres on such human evils as the Holocaust and Hiroshima. Of course, the difficult questions posed for theology by natural evils have not gone away, but, in comparison with the questions forced upon religious thought by all that 'man has made of man' they seem to have grown less urgent. At the same time, however, there appears in Voltaire a hint of what was to become a dominant motif of nineteenth- and twentieth-century renderings of the question of evil, a motif in which we can see the mark of the subjective turn in modern thought: outrage. For if the turn to the subject is often conceived primarily in epistemological terms, as in the Kantian reordering of the basic questions of metaphysics, this, as we have seen, is only one expression of a move that more fundamentally takes its point of departure from the lived experience of subjectivity, i.e. what it is to exist as a subject. It is on this basis that what I have called outrage is explicitly and sustainedly given its voice in discussions of evil. Rather than being seen – as previously by philosophers and religionists alike – as something needing to be quietened or silenced, outrage now came to be understood precisely as that which needed to be addressed and answered, as a fury and an anguish that would only go away when it had received satisfaction.

...

The image of the pot as not having the right to question the potter is deeply rooted in the monotheistic tradition. It is used by Paul to parry the question as to how those who reject Christ can be blamed, if faith itself is a gift of God, and Paul, in turn, is quoting back to Isaiah (Rom. 9.19–21; Isa. 29.16, 45.9). But whereas it seems to be self-evident to Paul and Isaiah that the analogy fits closely the human condition and that we are as dependent for our being on God as the pot is dependent on the potter, Voltaire points decisively to the disanalogy, a disanalogy that has to do precisely with our existence as conscious and self-conscious beings, and, above all, as beings who are self-conscious in their suffering. Such beings, he is saying, may, indeed must, question their maker and cry out against a fate that condemns them to a life of so much suffering. We are not dumb artefacts but sentient beings, and it would be a denial of humanity itself to forbid us to protest or answer back. The ability to do just this is integral to our being the kind of beings we are. His implication, moreover, is that for all the philosophical sophistication of contemporary theories concerning the relationships between causes and effect, possible worlds and the pre-established harmony of freedom and necessity, Leibniz and his fellow theodicists are essentially pushed back to the dogmatic position that because we cannot know the whole picture we have no right to enquire about it and must simply accept the limitation on our knowledge and the existence of truths above our reason.

This repudiation of a time-hallowed appeal to human frailty in face of ultimate questions and the assertion of the rights of the outraged sensibility of an existing, suffering, and thinking being is also evidenced by the re-emergence of another biblical motif in the modern discussion of evil: the appeal to the exemplary suffering of Job. Here, however, the biblical paradigm, far from being repudiated, is reinstated and rescued from the falsification it had endured for centuries in ecclesiastical teaching. In the teaching of the church, Job had become 'patient Job', a prime example of patient submission to suffering and, as such, a type of Christ. A moment in the story favoured in iconographic representation is that of the exchange between Job and his wife, when she tells him to curse the God who has brought so many troubles upon his head, and so to die, and Job replies, 'You are talking like a foolish woman. Shall we accept good from God and not trouble?' (Job 2.10), on which the text comments, 'Job did not sin in what he said.' However, this incident and these verses are scarcely representative of *Job* as a whole. No less vivid, and far more likely to impress themselves on a modern reader, are the long passages in which Job effectively seems to be taking his wife's advice, as in his speeches in Chapters 3, 6, 9–10, 12–14, 16–17, 19, 21, 23–4, 26–31, in which he rejects the counsel of his friends, who urge him to see his punishment as somehow merited or part of God's plan, and, instead, bewails the sheer agony of his existence, the inexplicability and injustice of God's actions and his own desire for extinction.

. . .

Throughout these speeches Job not only insists on his own misery and his right to express it honestly, he also brushes aside the arguments of his friends, theodicists to a man ('Your maxims are proverbs of ashes; your defences are defences of clay' (Job 13.12)), and claims that nothing short of a direct confrontation with God would give him satisfaction, fearful and impossible as such a thing might be: '. . . let the Almighty answer me' (Job 31.35) he concludes. Strangely, when God finally does appear it is to say that it is Job, after all, who has spoken well of him and not the friends.

. . .

Kierkegaard . . . wishes to reinstate the 'despairing language of passion' to the religious questioning of humanity's experience of evil, suggesting, with Job, that the task is not for us to become God's 'defenders', pleading the rightness or justice of God ('theodicy'), but by our questioning to create a situation in which God can, as it were – and whatever might be meant by such a thing – 'defend himself'. Such a strategy, of course, means that the believer is no longer obliged to come up with arguments or reasons for going on believing despite the fact of evil but must himself accept and embrace and make his own the voice of outrage, because anything less will fail to do justice to the human experience and the human need that the question of evil articulates.

. . .

Dostoevsky's *The Brothers Karamazov* . . . also gave definitive expression to the voice of moral and religious outrage in face of humanly enacted evil. Although it is now reasonably clear that Dostoevsky's intentions were to write from a standpoint of faith, the text itself is seamed by such a network of fault-lines that belief is at continual risk of subsidence into unbelief, and those (many) early readers who interpreted Dostoevsky as a post-Christian and post-religious writer were, in their way, responding to a real possibility of the texts themselves. . . .

Here I wish only to note the notorious 'rebellion' of Ivan Karamazov, declaimed by him to his younger brother, the novice-monk Alyosha. Here Ivan comes close to reversing the hypothesis he had propounded earlier in the novel: that if God does not exist, then everything is permitted, a word claimed by Sartre as anticipating the essential teaching of existentialism – precisely, perhaps, because of the implied reversal of the syllogism: that in a world in which, it seems, everything *is* permitted (because even the most unthinkable crimes do, in fact, occur), then God does not exist.

Ivan, however, does not claim that God does not exist. His argument is, rather, that the kind of evil that really is met with in our world is such as to render odious the belief in a final harmony or happy ending that could justify the course of world history. Even if there is a judgement and an eschatological fulfilment beyond history, world history itself can never be justified for having been the way it has, in fact, been. Interestingly, and importantly, although Ivan alludes to instances of large-scale massacres, his argument requires there to have been only one instance of innocent suffering . . .

. . .

This, as I have already suggested, may not be Dostoevsky's own last word. But, I also suggest, it is a key to a central element of the modern response to evil. Should we seek to rise above it, to acknowledge its force as an immediate gut reaction but nevertheless resist its claim to decide the whole argument? The question is not so easy. But, we know, the aim of thinking about God is not to make religion easy, but to learn to think the questions of religion in their truth and therefore also in their difficulty. And that means, sometimes, thinking the question with total commitment and passion and continuing to think it even when no answer comes. The difficulty is not just finding 'the answer' but deciding the ground on which the question of evil is properly to be asked, and it is precisely this difficulty that the voice of outrage will not let us evade. Immediate and passionate as it may be (and thus far 'irrational') it is also philosophically important, since it compels us to ask all the more carefully just what it is we are trying to do here and just what kind of thinking the encounter with evil calls for.

Fyodor Dostoyevsky, *The Brothers Karamazov,* **ET London, Penguin, 1958, Volume I, pp. 285–8**

Ivan was silent for a minute and his face suddenly became very sad.

'Listen to me: I took only children to make my case clearer. I don't say anything about the other human tears with which the earth is saturated from its crust to its centre – I have narrowed my subject on purpose. I am a bug and I acknowledge in all humility that I can't understand why everything has been arranged as it is. I suppose men themselves are to blame: they were given paradise, they wanted freedom and they stole the fire from heaven [*an allusion to the classical tale of Prometheus*], knowing perfectly well that they would become unhappy, so why should we pity them? Oh, all that my pitiful earthly Euclidean mind can grasp is that suffering exists, that no one is to blame, that effect follows cause, simply and directly, that everything flows and finds its level – but then this is only Euclidean nonsense. I know that and I refuse to live by it! What do I care that no one is to blame, that effect follows cause simply and directly and that I know it – I must have retribution or I shall destroy myself. And retribution not somewhere in the infinity of space and time, but here on earth, and so that I could see it myself. I was a believer, and I want to see for myself. And if I'm dead by that time, let them resurrect me, for if it all happens without me, it will be too unfair. Surely the reason for my suffering was not that I as well as my evil deeds and sufferings may serve as manure for some future harmony for someone else. I want to see with my own eyes the lion lie down with the lamb and the murdered man rise up and embrace his murderer. I want to be there when everyone suddenly finds out what it has all been for. All religions on earth are based on this desire, and I am a believer. But then there are the children, and what am I to do with them? That is the question I cannot answer. I repeat for the hundredth time – there are lots of questions, but I've only taken the children, for in their case it is clear beyond the shadow of a doubt what I have to say. Listen: if all have to suffer so as to buy eternal harmony by their suffering, what have the children to do with it – tell me, please? It is entirely incomprehensible why they, too should have to suffer and why they should have to buy harmony by their sufferings. Why should they, too, be used as dung for someone's future harmony? I understand solidarity in sin among men, I understand solidarity in retribution, too, but, surely, there can be no solidarity in sin with children, and if it is really true that they share their fathers' responsibility for all their fathers' crimes, then that truth is not, of course, of this world and it's incomprehensible to me. Some humorous fellow may say that it makes no difference since a child is bound to grow up and sin, but, then, he didn't grow up: he was torn to pieces by dogs at the age of eight. Oh, Alyosha, I'm not blaspheming! I understand, of course, what a cataclysm of the universe it will be when everything in heaven and on earth blends in one hymn of praise and everything that lives and has lived cries loud: "Thou art just, O Lord, for thy ways are revealed!" Then, indeed, the mother will embrace the torturer who had her child torn to pieces by his dogs, and all three will cry aloud: "Thou art just, O Lord!", and then, of course, the crown of knowledge will have been attained and everything will be explained. But there's the rub: for it is that I cannot accept. And while I'm on earth, I hasten to take my own measures. For, you see, Alyosha, it may really happen that if I live to that moment, or rise again to see it, I shall perhaps myself cry aloud with the rest, as I look at the mother embracing her child's torturer: "Thou art just, O Lord!" But I do not want to cry aloud then. While there's still time, I make haste to arm myself against it, and that is why I renounce higher harmony altogether. It is not worth one little tear of that tortured little girl who beat herself on the breast and prayed to her "dear, kind Lord" in the stinking privy with her unexpiated tears! It is not worth it, because her tears remained unexpiated. They must be expiated, for otherwise there can be no harmony. But how, how are you to expiate them? Is it possible? Not, surely, by their being avenged? But what do I want them avenged for? What do I want a hell for torturers for? What good can hell do if they have already been tortured to death? And what sort of harmony is it, if there is a hell? I want to forgive. I want to embrace. I don't want any more suffering. And if the sufferings of children go to make up the sum of sufferings which is necessary for the purchase of truth, then I say beforehand that the entire truth is not worth such a price. And, finally, I do not want a mother to embrace the torturer who had her child torn to pieces by his dogs! She has no right to forgive him! If she likes, she can forgive him for herself, she can forgive the torturer for the immeasurable suffering he has inflicted upon her as a mother; but she has no right to forgive him for the sufferings of her tortured child. She has no right to forgive the torturer for that, even if her child were to forgive him! And if that is so, if they have no right to forgive him, what becomes of the harmony? Is there in the whole world a being who could or would have the right to forgive? I don't want harmony. I don't want it, out of the love I bear to mankind. I want to remain with my suffering unavenged. I'd rather remain with my suffering unavenged and my indignation unappeased, *even if I were wrong*. Besides, too high a price has been placed on harmony. We cannot afford to pay so much for admission. And therefore I hasten to return my ticket of admission. And indeed, if I am an honest man, I'm bound to hand it back as soon as possible. This I am doing. It is not God that I do not accept, Alyosha. I merely most respectfully return him the ticket.'

'This is rebellion,' Alyosha said softly, dropping his eyes.

'Rebellion? I'm sorry to hear you say that,' Ivan said with feeling. 'One can't go on living in a state of rebellion, and I want to live. Tell me frankly, I appeal to you – answer me: imagine that it is you yourself who are erecting the edifice of human destiny with the aim of making men happy in the end, of giving them peace and contentment at last, but that to do that it is absolutely necessary, and indeed quite inevitable, to torture to death only one tiny creature, the little girl who beat her breast with her little fist, and to found the edifice on her unavenged tears – would you consent to be the architect on those conditions? Tell me and do not lie!'

'No, I wouldn't,' Alyosha said softly.

'And can you admit the idea that the people for whom you are building it would agree to accept their happiness at the price of the unjustly shed blood of a little tortured child and having accepted it, to remain forever happy?'

'No, I can't admit it. Ivan,' Alyosha said suddenly with flashing eyes, 'you said just now, is there a being in the whole world who could or had the right to forgive? But there is such a being, and he can forgive everything, everyone and everything and *for everything*, because he gave his innocent blood for all and for everything. You've forgotten him, but it is on him that the edifice is founded, and it is to him that they will cry aloud: "Thou art just, O Lord, for thy ways are revealed!"'

1.2 Theodicy and bad faith

Kenneth Surin, *Theology and the Problem of Evil*, Oxford, Blackwell, 1986, pp. 51–2, 83–4

The most terrible visions are conjured up by certain names: the Warsaw ghetto, Auschwitz, the Gulag, the refugee camps of Beirut, Biafra, Pol Pot's 'Year Zero', and so forth. The evil perpetrated in these places and at these times was not abstract: 'annihilation is no longer a metaphor. Good and evil are real'. The evil deeds associated with these places and times were of such a malignant and palpable magnitude that some writers, Sartre for example, have been moved to assert that evil is irredeemable:

> We have been taught to take [evil] seriously. It is neither our fault nor our merit if we live in a time when torture was a daily fact . . . Dachau and Auschwitz . . . have demonstrated to us that Evil is not an appearance, that knowing its cause does not dispel it, that it is not opposed to Good as a confused idea is to a clear one, that it is not the effect of passions which might be cured, of a fear which might be overcome, of a passing aberration which might be excused, of an ignorance which might be enlightened . . .

We heard whole streets screaming and understood that Evil . . . is like Good, absolute.

Perhaps a day will come when a happy age, looking back at the past, will see in this suffering and shame one of the paths to peace. But we were not on the side of history already made. We were, as I have said, *situated* in such a way that every minute seemed to us like something irreducible. Therefore, in spite of ourselves, we came to this conclusion, which will seem shocking to lofty souls: Evil cannot be redeemed. (*What is Literature?*, 1950, pp. 160–2)

A theodicist who, intentionally or inadvertently, formulates doctrines which occlude the radical and ruthless particularity of human evil is, by implication, mediating a social and political practice which averts its gaze from the cruelties that exist in the world. The theodicist, we are suggesting, cannot propound views that promote serenity in a heartless world. If she does, her words will be dissipated in the ether of abstract moralizing, and she will become like the persons described by Joseph Conrad in his great short story 'An Outpost of Progress', who 'talk with indignation and enthusiasm; talk about oppression, cruelty, crime, devotion, self-sacrifice, virtue, and . . . know nothing real beyond the words. Nobody knows what suffering or sacrifice mean – except perhaps the victims'.

Theodicy, then, has to engage with the sheer particularity, the radical contingency, of human evil. The theodicist cannot, of course, guarantee that her doctrines will have any real or immediate import for *the victims* of such evil, but she must at least not attempt to disengage herself from their plight by adhering to a viewpoint of specious generality, which effectively reduces theodicy to mere ideology, and which in the process merely reinforces the powerlessness of those who are powerless. If, as Conrad says, only the victims can truly understand what suffering and sacrifice mean, then theodicy must necessarily be articulated from the standpoint of the victims themselves. Otherwise, theodicy will succumb inevitably to what Paul Ricoeur calls 'the bad faith of theodicy': 'it does not triumph over real evil but only over its aesthetic phantom'. A theodicy is not worth heeding if it does not allow the screams of our society to be heard.

. . .

Even the screams of the innocent further the purposes of this (Swinburnean) God [*Richard Swinburne, a strong advocate of the free will defence, argues that God may know that 'the suffering that A will cause*

B is not nearly as great as B's screams might suggest to us and will provide (unknown to us) an opportunity to C to help B recover and will thus give C a deep responsibility which he would otherwise not have']. D. Z. Phillips says that 'to ask of what use are the screams of the innocent, as Swinburne's defense would have us do, is to embark on a speculation we should not even contemplate', and that to speculate thus 'is a sign of a corrupt mind'. In [his] reply to Phillips, Swinburne contends that

> when we are doing philosophy and are justified in doing so (as I hope that we are now) it is *never* a 'sign of a corrupt mind' to be open-minded about things. In all areas of life what seems most obviously true sometimes turns out to be false, and it is not the sign of a corrupt mind but the sign of a seeker after truth to examine carefully views which initially seem obviously true. It seemed obvious to many men that the Earth was flat; we may, however, be grateful that despite this, they were prepared to listen to arguments to the contrary. (In S. C. Brown (ed.), *Reason and Religion*, Ithaca, NY, Cornell University Press, 1977, pp. 92, 130)

It *is* precisely the sign of a corrupt mind to speak easily of two different realities, say, the world of the Flat Earth Society on the one hand and the world of Auschwitz on the other, as if they are interchangeable. To be 'open-minded' about certain realities, and 'more tellingly' to *insist* on retaining such a contemplative disposition, is to show oneself to be incapable of making certain exigent moral discriminations. In the worst cases, this incapacity to acknowledge that a particular reality is mind-stopping betokens an irremissable moral blindness, in less serious occurrences it testifies to a real lack of moral imagination, to an unshakeable moral coarseness. But in *all* cases the failure to lend a voice to the cries of the innocent (and there can be few more glaring instances of this failure than the willingness to construct a divine teleology out of innocent suffering) is to have lost the capacity to tell the truth: 'The need to lend a voice to suffering is a condition of all truth. For suffering is objectivity that weighs upon the subject . . .'

In cases where human beings are *in extremis*, to be 'open-minded', and thus to deafen one's ears to their cries, is to repudiate their flesh-and-bloodness, their being human. And in this hedging of one's acknowledgement of the humanity of the other, one has lost one's own humanity.

1.3 Finding God in evil

Elie Wiesel, *Night*, ET London, Penguin, 1981, pp. 76–7

One day when we came back from work, we saw three gallows rearing up in the assembly place . . .

The SS seemed more preoccupied, more disturbed than usual. To hang a young boy in front of thousands of spectators was no light matter.

. . .

The three victims mounted together on to the chairs.
The three necks were placed at the same moment within the nooses.
'Long live liberty!' cried the two adults.
But the child was silent.
'Where is God? Where is He?' someone behind me asked.
At a sign from the head of the camp, the three chairs tipped over.
Total silence throughout the camp. On the horizon, the sun was setting.
'Bare your heads!' yelled the head of the camp. His voice was raucous. We were weeping.
'Cover your heads!'
Then the march past began. The two adults were no longer alive. Their tongues hung swollen, blue-tinged. But the third rope was still moving; being so light, the child was still alive . . .

For more than half an hour he stayed there, struggling between life and death, dying in slow agony under our eyes. And we had to look him full in the face. He was still alive when I passed in front of him. His tongue was still red, his eyes were not yet glazed.

Behind me, I heard the same man asking:
'Where is God now?'
And I heard a voice within me answer him:
'Where is He? Here He is – He is hanging here on this gallows . . . .'

1.4 Protest atheism and the cross

Jürgen Moltmann, *The Crucified God: The Cross of Christ as the Foundation and Criticism of Christian Theology*, ET London: SCM, 1974, pp. 273–4, 219–22, 226–7

A shattering expression of the *theologia crucis* [theology of the cross] which is suggested in the rabbinic theology of God's humiliation of himself is to be found in *Night*, a book written by E. Wiesel, a survivor of Auschwitz:

. . .

'Where is God now?' And I heard a voice in myself answer: 'Where is he? He is here. He is hanging there on the gallows . . .'

Any other answer would be blasphemy. There cannot be any other Christian answer to the question of this torment. To speak here of a God who could not suffer would make God a demon. To speak here of an absolute God would make God an annihilating nothingness. To speak here of an indifferent God would condemn men to indifference.

. . .

Atheism, too, draws a conclusion from the existence of the finite world as it is to its cause and destiny. But there it finds no good and righteous God, but a capricious demon, a blind destiny, a damning law or an annihilating nothingness. As long as this world is not 'God-coloured', it does not allow any conclusions to God's existence, righteousness, wisdom and goodness. Thus, as the world has really been made, belief in the devil is much more plausible than belief in God. The hells of world wars, the hells of Auschwitz, Hiroshima and Vietnam, and also the everyday experiences which make one man say to another 'You make my life hell', often suggest that the world as a whole should be thought of as a 'house of the dead', a house of discipline, a madhouse or a *univers concentrationnaire*, and not the good earth under the gracious heaven of a righteous God. Strindberg declared: 'Jesus Christ descended to hell, but his descent was his wandering here on earth, his way of suffering through the madhouse, the house of discipline, the mortuary of this earth.' In Schiller's 'Ode to Joy' we find:

> Be patient, O millions!
> Be patient for the better world!
> There above the starry sky
> A great God will give a reward.

Against this theodicy of German idealism, in Dostoevsky's novel Ivan Karamazov tells a story of a poor serf child who hit his master's hunting dog with a stone while he was playing. The master had him seized and the next morning he was hunted and torn to pieces by the master's hounds before his mother's eyes.

. . .

This is the classical form of *protest atheism*. The question of the existence of God is, in itself, a minor issue in the face of the question of his righteousness in the world. And this question of suffering and revolt is not answered by any cosmological argument for the existence of God or any theism, but is rather provoked by both of these. If one argues back from the state of the world and the fact of its existence to cause, ground and principle, one can just as well speak of 'God' as of the devil, of being as of nothingness, of the meaning of the world as of absurdity. Thus the history of Western atheism becomes at the same time the history of nihilism. In this atheistic, de-divinized world, literature is full of the 'monotheism of Satan' and the mythologoumena of evil. It varies the images: God as deceiver, executioner, sadist, despot, player, director of a marionette theatre – or it introduces the images of the sleeping, erring, bored, helpless and clownish God. 'I would not want to be God at the present moment.' These blasphemies are fundamentally provocations of God, for there is something that the atheist fears over and above all torments. That is the indifference of God and his final retreat from the world of men.

Here atheism demonstrates itself to be the brother of theism. It too makes use of logical inference. It too sees the world as the mirror of another, higher being. With just as much justification as that with which theism speaks of God, the highest, best, righteous being, it speaks of the nothingness which manifests itself in all the annihilating experiences of suffering and evil. It is the inescapable antithesis of theism. But if metaphysical theism disappears, can protest atheism still remain alive? For its protest against injustice and death, does not it need an authority to accuse, because it makes this authority responsible for the state of affairs? And can it make this authority responsible if it has not previously declared it to be behind the way in which the world is and exists? Following Dostoevsky, Camus called this atheism a 'metaphysical rebellion'. It is 'the means by which a man protests against his condition and against the whole of creation. It is metaphysical because it disputes the ends of man and of creation.' According to Camus, the metaphysical rebellion does not derive from Greek tragedy but from the Bible, with its concept of the personal God. 'The history of the rebellion that we experience today is far more that of the descendants of Cain than the pupils of Prometheus [*i.e. the protest derives from Hebrew rather than Greek thought*]. In this sense, it is above all others the God of the Old Testament who sets in motion the energies of the rebellion.'

. . .

Crude atheism for which this world is everything is as superficial as the theism which claims to prove the existence of God from the reality of this world. Protest atheism points beyond both God and suffering, suffering and God, sets them one against the other and becomes an atheistic protest against injustice 'for God's sake'. In the context of the question which sets God and suffering over against each other, a God who sits enthroned in heaven in a glory that no one can share is unacceptable even for theology. Equally so, a grief which only affects man externally and does not seize him and change him in his very person does not do it justice. But in that case must not Christian theology take up once again the old theopaschite question 'Did God himself suffer?', in order to be able to think of God not in absolute terms, in the usual way, but in particular terms as in Christ? Before it can talk of the significance of the history of Christ's suffering for the history of the world's suffering, Christian theology must have faced the intrinsic problem of the history of Christ's suffering and have understood God's being in the godforsakenness of Christ. Only when it has recognized what took place between Jesus and his Father on the cross can it speak of the significance of this God for those who suffer and protest at the history of the world.

The only way past protest atheism is through a theology of the cross which understands God as the suffering God in the suffering of Christ and which cries out with the godforsaken God, 'My God, why have you forsaken me?' For this theology, God and suffering are no longer contradictions, as in theism and atheism, but God's being is in suffering and the suffering is in God's being itself, because God is love. It takes the 'metaphysical rebellion' up into itself because it recognizes in the cross of Christ a rebellion in metaphysics, or better, a rebellion in God himself: God himself loves and suffers the death of Christ in his love. He is no 'cold heavenly power', nor does he 'tread his way over corpses', but is know as the human God in the crucified Son of Man.

A. Roy Eckardt, 'Jürgen Moltmann, the Jewish People and the Holocaust', *Journal of the American Academy of Religion*, XLIV, 4, 1976, pp. 683–5, 687

Separate attention may be given to Jürgen Moltmann's allusion to Elie Wiesel and its immediate sequel. Part of the famous episode from *Night* is reproduced (pp. 273–274): a youth is hanged at a death camp, and a voice whispers that God is hanging there on the gallows. Moltmann offers the response, 'Any other answer would be blasphemy. There cannot be any other *Christian* answer to the question of this torment' (emphasis added). But why has the word 'Christian' been inserted here?

The sufferer was a Jew. Further, the voice giving the answer is that of a Jew. However, a much more shattering consideration is involved: It may be asked why the section, 'The fullness of life in the trinitarian history of God,' is given a location immediately after the story from *Night* (pp. 274ff.). An element of 'blasphemy' appears, however unintended this may be. The reputed restrictiveness within Judaism that Moltmann constructs here does not meet the command of love for the sufferers. He moves quickly from the tale of the youth's hanging into a theological disputation between Christian theology and Jewish theology. Thus, for example, 'only in and through Christ' is the 'dialogical relationship with God opened up.' And again, 'no relationship of immediacy between God and man is conceivable' that is separated from the person of Christ. Reference is made to the church as the 'universal community' of God, in explicit opposition to Jewish 'particularism.' It is sad that Moltmann says these things *at this place* in his study. We plead only for respect for the dead children, women, and men who could never accept such propositions as those just cited. Let us enable the sufferers of Auschwitz to have their moment alone with God, or without him, and not intrude with our theological caveats, however much these may arise from conscience and conviction. Picture a Christian representative standing next to that gallows in Buna, in the presence of the lad in torment, and reading aloud pp. 275 and 276 of *The Crucified God*. . . . Would it not be infinitely more fitting just to honor these persons as human beings, and let the matter stand that way?

. . .

The foregoing materials lead to a rudimentary effort at theological reconstruction . . . Two fundamental and interrelated issues may be raised: first, the historical-moral fate of the cross as a religious symbol, taken in the context of the fate of the Jewish people; and, second, the theological-moral question of the advocated link between the cross and ultimate horribleness.

(1) . . . The 'crucified Christ' simply cannot be separated from what has happened to, and been done to, the cross. Moltmann maintains that 'the cross does not divide Christians from Jews' (p. 134). In truth, untold numbers of Jews cannot distinguish the cross from the *Hakenkreuz* [*hooked cross, i.e. swastika*]. It was after the Holocaust that a Jewish woman, catching sight of a huge cross displayed in New York City each year at Christmastime, said to her walking companion, Edward H. Flannery, 'That cross makes me shudder. It is like an evil presence.' It was in

and through the Holocaust that the symbol of the cross became ultimately corrupted by devilishness. When asked by two bishops in 1933 what he was going to do about the Jews, Adolf Hitler replied that he would do to them exactly what the church had been advocating and practicing for almost two thousand years.

. . .

(2) . . . Moltmann adjudges that due to Jesus' 'full consciousness that God is close at hand in his grace,' his abandonment and deliverance up to death, as one rejected, is the very torment of hell, and puts at stake the very deity of Jesus' God and Father (pp. 148, 151). I suggest that this particular 'abomination of desolation' simply does not stand up as the absolute horror upon which Christian faith then can and should, dialectically, build its hope. I contend that in comparison with certain other sufferings, Jesus' death becomes non-decisive.

. . .

It may be suggested to Professor Moltmann that there is an evil in this world which is more terrible than every other evil, in every time and in every place. This is the evil of little children witnessing the murders of other little children, *while knowing that they also are to be murdered in the same way, being aware absolutely that they face the identical fate*. Before this kind of event, the death of Jesus upon the cross fades into comparative moral triviality. At most, its advocacy reflects pre-Holocaust theology; it is not theology 'after Auschwitz.' Its Godforsakenness proves to be non-ultimate, for there is now a Godforsakenness that is worse by an infinity of infinities.

1.5 Suffering and the death of Christ

John Barton, *Love Unknown: Meditations on the Death and Resurrection of Jesus,* **London, SPCK, 1990, pp. 14–17**

Jesus' life was not the unfolding of a prearranged set of events, all neatly shaped to point towards the passion. Indeed, the Gospels, for all their artistic structure, do not really give that impression. They are full of incidents that just happened, and could equally well have happened otherwise. There have been Christian schemes of thought which have seen the events of Jesus' life (and for that matter all the events in the history of the world) as foreordained by God, eliminating all chance and all randomness. But the Bible, taken by and large, does not support this way of thinking. The story it tells is full of muddle, inconsequential in places, and with surprises on every page; and the life of Jesus is no exception to this. Jesus was not speaking the lines of a script or obeying the directions of an invisible producer; he was living from day to day, just as we have to, with no certainty of what the future held – though undoubtedly with a foreboding that, if he insisted on sticking to the style of life and teaching to which he was committed, suffering and death could scarcely be avoided. That is a long way from saying starkly, 'Jesus was born to die.'

. . .

Jesus did not get himself executed. The contingencies of expressing God's love for his people in the only way it could be expressed, in the very particular circumstances in which he happened to be, turned out to lead to collision with the authorities, and so to trial and execution. There was no 'must' about it, except the compulsion of divine love to be true to itself whatever happens. My colleague David Brown puts it like this:

> . . . note . . . the arbitrariness of the form of Jesus' death. Had he lived a few centuries earlier and lived in a different land it might have taken the relatively painless form of drinking hemlock, as with Socrates. Again, were it to have taken place this century in some of the countries of Latin America, it could well have been much more gruesome still – years of torture producing a wasted body that is finally just dumped in an anonymous grave . . . One might even be prepared to go further, and question whether the story had to end brutally [at all]. For it is not so much the fact of the suffering itself that produces its impact on us, as the way in which Jesus responded to the diverse actors in the story as the drama unfolded . . . God's involvement with suffering in Christ is an involvement with that most frightening aspect of suffering, its essential arbitrariness . . . It is this which makes Christ's cry of dereliction from the cross the cry of all sufferers – Why me? Why has God abandoned me to this fate? . . . Here in Jesus we have God himself endorsing that cry, the tragic element in his creation that each new sufferer must discover for himself, that there is no reason why it has befallen him rather than another . . . It is no part of the divine plan that any specific individual suffer pain. But because pain is a tragic consequence of the values the creation embodies, God has chosen to enter into our pain at its most acute and now is always available to help creatively transform whatever befalls us as one who knew pain at its worst and potentially

most destructive. (In R. Morgan (ed.), *The Religion of the Incarnation*, Bristol, Bristol Classical Press, 1989, pp. 54–7)

Christians have not been good at grasping this 'arbitrariness' in the story of their Lord's suffering and death – it has sounded too much like saying that God was not in control. But unless we do grasp it, we shall always run the risk of worshipping a God who did not *quite* share our humanity, but always held something – indeed, the most crucial thing – back.

Dorothee Soelle, *Suffering*, ET London, Darton, Longman & Todd, 1975, pp. 148–9

The decisive phrase, that God is hanging 'here on this gallows,' has two meanings. First, it is an assertion about God. God is no executioner – and no almighty spectator (which would amount to the same thing). God is not the mighty tyrant. Between the sufferer and the one who causes the suffering, between the victim and the executioner, God, whatever people make of this word, is on the side of the sufferer. God is on the side of the victim, he is hanged.

Second, it is an assertion about the boy. If it is not also an assertion about the boy, then the story is false and one can forget about the first assertion. But how can the assertion about the boy be made without cynicism? 'He is with God, he has been raised, he is in heaven.' Such traditional phrases are almost always clerical cynicism with a high apathy content. Sometimes one stammers such phrases which are in fact true as a child repeats something he doesn't understand, with confidence in the speaker and the language that has still not become part of him. That is always possible, but in the long run it destroys those who do it because learning to believe also means learning to speak, and it is theologically necessary to transcend the shells of our inherited language. What language can possibly serve not only to preserve for all the life asserted by classical theology but primarily to translate it into a language of liberation? We would have to learn to hear the confession of the Roman centurion, 'Truly this was God's son,' in the phrase, 'Here he is – he is hanging here on this gallows.' Every single one of the six million was God's beloved son. Were anything else the case, resurrection would not have occurred, even in Jesus' case.

God is not in heaven; he is hanging on the cross. Love is not an otherworldly, intruding, self-asserting power – and to meditate on the cross can mean to take leave of that dream.

Precisely those who in suffering experience the strength of the weak, who incorporate the suffering into their lives, for whom coming through free of suffering is no longer the highest goal, precisely they are there for the others who, with no choice in the matter, are crucified in lives of senseless suffering. A different salvation, as the language of metaphysics could promise it, is no longer possible. The God who causes suffering is not to be justified even by lifting the suffering later. No heaven can rectify Auschwitz. But the God who is not a greater Pharaoh has justified himself: in sharing the suffering, in sharing the death on the cross.

Doctrine Commission of the General Synod of the Church of England, *We Believe in God,* **London, Church House Publishing, 1991, pp. 157–9, 160–1**

The idea that God loves his creatures as a father loves his children and consequently suffers when his creatures fail to respond to that love is at the heart of the Christian understanding of God. It was 'through Christ' that God reconciled the world to himself – and Christ suffered and died upon the Cross, as a result of the failure of the world to acknowledge and respond to God's love. So, it would appear, God suffered; and if so, our model suggests that he may continue to suffer whenever his creatures reject his purposes for them, somewhat as a human father suffers when his children reject his loving care for them.

Moreover, this way of understanding God's relationship with his creatures enables believers to confront the problem of evil with a new confidence. Again and again, human beings are subjected to suffering, sometimes in consequence of their own sinfulness, sometimes as victims of totally (as it seems) unmerited and inexplicable calamities. Why, they cry, does God allow this to happen? The beginning of an answer may be found, as we have seen, in the notion of constraints inherent in any act of creation; given that God used his freedom to create a world that would be an appropriate environment for free, adventurous and potentially loving human beings, he accepted the constraints imposed upon him by that creative activity, and is therefore not free to obviate all the consequences which cause us to suffer (though, in answer to prayer, he may obviate some). But the father-model is also capable of suggesting a more profound and ultimately far more sustaining answer. Just as a human father suffers if the circumstances in which he has deliberately placed his children for their good turn out to cause them suffering, so we may say that God suffers because of the sufferings of his creatures. We may even say that God is so 'involved' in their suffering that he is actually 'in' the suffering itself. Many Christians would say that it was precisely by coming to grasp and experience this presence of God within human suffering that they have been enabled to bear it and accept it themselves.

But at this point serious misgivings arise. Have we pushed the use of our model too far? Certain things, we believe, must be true of God; otherwise he ceases to be God at all. If we are to attribute suffering to God, must he not cease to be permanent and unchangeable? Does not the believer, struggling against evil and sorrow, require a God who is strong, trustworthy and constant?

There is a technical name in theology for the doctrine which meets this requirement: the impassibility of God. According to this, God by his very nature cannot suffer; and if our father-son model has led us to say something which traditional doctrine explicitly excludes from consideration we must be prepared to abandon it. But in fact this doctrine requires closer examination. If it is to be taken to mean that God does not suffer as we suffer, what becomes of the person of the incarnate Christ? Are we to say that his human nature obviously suffered mental and physical agony, but that the divine nature (i.e. the Word united to the human nature) was somehow anaesthetised by virtue of the simple fact that divinity cannot suffer? But this is to make a nonsense of what the Christian tradition is saying about the person of Christ. Certainly the classical position (as enunciated, for example, at the Council of Chalcedon) is that the two natures in Christ – human and divine – are distinct. But it also states that the two natures are united in one single person and that therefore if Christ suffered then the whole Christ suffered.

It could of course be said (as in the Theopaschite controversy of the sixth century) that this was God temporarily dipping his toes in the waters of human anguish. 'One of the Trinity suffered', but not for long, while the Father and the Spirit remained as aloof as before. But to say this is to distort the doctrine of the Trinity, to fly in the face of the truth that the three Persons are as inseparable in their nature as they are in their creative and redemptive activity. If one suffers, then all suffer, or better, if God is in Christ suffering for our redemption, then this is the sign and guarantee of the Triune God's eternal involvement in human suffering and human destiny. For authentically Christian speech about God is always speech about the Holy Trinity. To think about God's relation to suffering simply in terms of the Father and the Son as separate Beings with different 'histories' (and to leave out the Spirit altogether) is not thinking about the Christian God at all.

Equally false to a Trinitarian vision of God, however, is any treatment of the Persons of the Trinity as if they were replicas of one another, so that whatever we say about the Incarnate Son can be said in the same terms about the Father. The Letter to the Hebrews, for example, says that the Son 'learned obedience through the things that he suffered' (5.8). Any doctrine of genuine Incarnation must say something of this sort. But Christians, at least in the mainstream traditions, do not say that God as God has to go through suffering in order to learn, develop or mature. In God, the wholeness of divine perfection has always been there, and is being brought to bear upon the cosmic drama of pain and evil. It is of the Incarnate Son, sharing in human existence within Space–Time, that we can properly say that he experienced the authentic process of growth into human wholeness, albeit with the appropriate perfection at each stage.

. . .

But the Christian faith is not just that, in Christ, the burden of suffering and evil in the world is shared by the Triune God in his love and compassion. In the Resurrection, it has been decisively overcome.

. . .

It is . . . precisely because they are Christ's Body in this world, baptised into the pattern of his death and resurrection, that Christians are those who enter into the long-suffering patience of God, sharing his victory over evil by absorbing it in inexhaustible forgiveness, and waiting with him in sure and certain hope of the ultimate triumph of love. The nature of this triumph is revealed unmistakably in the Gospel stories of the first Easter Day. Jesus returns to his friends in a new and transcendent life and power; but the love and forgiveness that marked his early existence are unchanged, and the Risen Body still bears the scars and wounds of the Crucified . . . In the hands of the divine artist what went 'wrong' has become the central and distinctive feature of an even greater work: 'See my hands and my feet, that it is I, myself.'

The Resurrection does not cancel or merely redress the truth that shines from the cross; it confirms it. This is the eternal nature of divine power and victory, insofar as our human minds are capable of grasping it.

This God does not promise that we shall be protected from the accidents and ills of this life, but that those who open themselves to him will be empowered with the human resources of endurance, insight and selflessness that can turn misfortune to good account. The well-known words of Phil. 4.13 in the older versions, 'I can do all things through Christ who strengthens me', are in fact a misleading rendering. The truer sense, which is also more appropriate in the context, is, 'I have strength to cope with anything'.

1.6 Survival, endurance and the Holocaust

Dan Cohn-Sherbok, 'Jewish Faith and the Holocaust', *Religious Studies*, 26, 2, 1990, pp. 289–90, 292–3

Though the Bible [*the Jewish Bible, i.e. the Old Testament*] only contains faint references to the realm of the dead, the doctrine of Life after Death came into prominence during the Maccabean period when righteous individuals were dying for their faith. Subsequently the belief in the World to Come was regarded as one of the central tenets of the Jewish faith. According to rabbinic scholars, it was inconceivable that life would end at death: God's justice demanded that the righteous of Israel enter into a realm of eternal bliss where they would be compensated for their earthly travail. Because of this belief generations of Jews have been able to reconcile their belief in a benevolent and merciful God with the terrible tragedies they have endured. Through the centuries the conviction that the righteous would inherit eternal life has sustained generations of Jewish martyrs who suffered persecution and death. As Jews were slaughtered, they glorified God through dedication to the Jewish faith – such an act is referred to as *Kiddush ha-Shem* (Sanctification of the Divine Name). These heroic Jews who remained steadfast in their faith did not question the ways of God; rather their deaths testify to their firm belief in a providential Lord of history who would reserve a place for them in the Hereafter.

. . .

When confronted by force, Jews attempted to defend themselves, but chose death if this proved impossible. Thousands of Jews in the Middle Ages lost their lives. Some fell in battle, but the majority committed suicide for their faith. In the chronicles of this slaughter *Kiddush ha-Shem* was the dominant motif; Jews endeavoured to fight their assailants, but when their efforts failed they died as martyrs.

. . .

Without the eventual vindication of the righteous in Paradise, there is no way to sustain the belief in a providential God who watches over His chosen people. The essence of the Jewish understanding of God is that He loves His chosen people. If death means extinction, there is no way to make sense of the claim that He loves and cherishes all those who died in the concentration camps – suffering and death would ultimately triumph over each of those who perished. But if there is eternal life in a World to Come, then there is hope that the righteous will share in a divine life. Moreover, the divine attribute of justice demands that the righteous of Israel who met their death as innocent victims of the Nazis will reap an everlasting reward. Here then is an answer to the religious perplexities of the Holocaust. The promise of immortality offers a way of reconciling the belief in a loving and just God with the nightmare of the death camps.

Emil L. Fackenheim, 'The 614th Commandment', in Emil L. Fackenheim, *The Jewish Return into History: Reflections in the Age of Auschwitz and a New Jerusalem*, New York, Schocken Books, 1978, pp. 22–4

Can we confront the Holocaust, and yet not despair? Not accidentally has it taken twenty years for us to face this question, and it is not certain that we can face it yet. The contradiction is too staggering, and every authentic escape is barred. *For we are forbidden to turn present and future life into death, as the price of remembering death at Auschwitz. And we are equally forbidden to affirm present and future life, at the price of forgetting Auschwitz.*

We have lived in this contradiction for twenty years without being able to face it. Unless I am mistaken, we are now beginning to face it, however fragmentarily and inconclusively. And from this beginning confrontation there emerges what I will boldly term a 614th commandment: *the authentic Jew of today is forbidden to hand Hitler yet another, posthumous victory*. (This formulation is terribly inadequate, yet I am forced to use it until one more adequate is found. First, although no anti-Orthodox implication is intended, as though the 613 commandments stood necessarily in need of change, we must face the fact that something radically new has happened. Second, although the commandment should be positive rather than negative, we must face the fact that Hitler did win at least one victory – the murder of six million Jews. Third, although the very name of Hitler should be erased rather than remembered, we cannot disguise the uniqueness of his evil under a comfortable generality, such as persecution-in-general, tyranny-in-general, or even the demonic-in-general.)

I think the authentic Jew of today is beginning to hear the 614th commandment. And he hears it whether, as agnostic, he hears no more, or whether, as believer, he hears the voice of the *metzaveh* (the commander) in the *mitzvah* (the commandment). Moreover, it may well be the case that the authentic Jewish agnostic and the authentic Jewish believer are closer today than at any previous time.

. . .

If the 614th commandment is binding upon the authentic Jew, then we are, first, commanded to survive as Jews, lest the Jewish people perish. We are commanded, second, to remember in our very guts and bones the martyrs of the Holocaust, lest their memory perish. We are forbidden, thirdly, to deny or despair of God, however much we may have to contend with him or with belief in him, lest Judaism perish. We are forbidden, finally, to despair of the world as the place which is to become the kingdom of God, lest we help make it a meaningless place in which God is dead or irrelevant and everything is permitted. To abandon any of these imperatives, in response to Hitler's victory at Auschwitz, would be to hand him yet other, posthumous victories.

How can we possibly obey these imperatives? To do so requires the endurance of intolerable contradictions. Such endurance cannot but bespeak an as yet unutterable faith. If we are capable of this endurance, then the faith implicit in it may well be of historic consequence. At least twice before – at the time of the destruction of the First and of the Second Temples – Jewish endurance in the midst of catastrophe helped transform the world. We cannot know the future, if only because the present is without precedent. But this ignorance on our part can have no effect on our present action. The uncertainty of what will be may not shake our certainty of what we must do.

Immanuel Jakobovits, ' "Faith, Ethics and the Holocaust": Some Personal, Theological and Religious Responses to the Holocaust', *Holocaust and Genocide Studies*, 3, 4, 1988, p. 372

Would it not be a catastrophic perversion of the Jewish spirit if brooding over the Holocaust were to become a substantial element in the Jewish purpose, and if the anxiety to prevent another Holocaust were to be relied upon as an essential incentive to Jewish activity? I fear that this mood is already widespread, in our propaganda as well as in our philosophy. Should we not rather replace negative by positive factors to vindicate our claim to survival? The slogan 'Never again!', now so popular, is a poor substitute for purposeful Jewish living as a potent driving force to promote Jewish vitality. We exist not in order to prevent our own destruction, but to advance our special assignment, embodying the ageless values which are our natural *raison d'être*. We must shift the current emphasis on the survival of Jews to the survival of Judaism. For without Judaism, Jewish survival is both questionable and meaningless.

To me, the *meaning* of being a Jew has not changed with Auschwitz. What has changed is that millions of Jews are now threatened by self-liquidation even more so than by oppression, and it is this threat which the legacy of the Holocaust summons us to counter with unprecedented urgency and vigour.

A. Roy Eckardt, 'Salient Christian-Jewish Issues of Today: A Christian Exploration', in J. H. Charlesworth (ed.), *Jews and Christians: Exploring the Past, Present, and Future*, New York, Crossroad, 1990, pp. 159–60

The political dimension is already identified as decisive in and through the foregoing discussion on theodicy. A few citations will help fill out the point. These are from an essay by Alice L. Eckardt titled 'Power and Powerlessness: The Jewish Experience.'

. . .

> [The] silence of Auschwitz underlines the fact that hope without power is not a hopeful position in a world where power dominates, in a world that has seen all too clearly the price of powerlessness. . . .
>
> Those conclusions that most Jews have reached, along with some Christians who have understood the absolute challenge that the Holocaust continues to represent, include: an insistence that the end of Jewish statelessness . . . is a responsible religious and political commitment; that forces of death and destruction – radical evil – must be resisted on behalf of life and a community's existence . . . ; that martyrdom can no longer be either the ideal religious or the responsible political method of responding to tyranny or other forms of evil; that peace and community must be the continual goal of our strivings, but not at the expense of a 'sacrificial offering' of some one nation or people. It is time for the Jewish 'return into history' with all the responsibilities and ambiguities – and mistakes – of power and decision-making that this entails, and all the courage that it requires.

The political-moral judgment upon Christians today centers upon the question: Do you or do you not affirm Jewish power, Jewish national sovereignty? If you do not, how is it possible for you to escape enlistment in 'the ranks of those who would like to repeat the Holocaust'?

Johann-Baptist Metz, 'Facing the Jews: Christian Theology after Auschwitz', *Concilium*, 175, 1984 (Elisabeth Schüssler Fiorenza and David Tracy (eds), *The Holocaust as Interruption*, Edinburgh, T & T Clark), pp. 29–30

Who really has the right to give the answer to the God-question – 'Where is God? Here he is – he hangs on the gallows'? Who, if anyone at all, has the right to give it? As far as I am concerned, only the Jew threatened by death with all the children in Auschwitz has the right to say it – only he alone. There is no other 'identification' of God – neither as sublime as for instance in J. Moltmann nor as reserved and modest as in the case of D. Sölle – here, as far as I am concerned, no Christian-theological identification of God is possible. If at all, this can be done only by the Jew imprisoned together with his God in the abyss ... Only he, I think, can alone speak of a 'God on the gallows', not we Christians outside of Auschwitz who sent the Jew into such a situation of despair or at least left him in it.

Topics for discussion

1 Are there any important differences between not believing in God and not believing in a particular type of God?
2 Are theologians fair when they accuse philosophers of being callous in their approach to the problem of suffering? To what extent are the philosopher and theologian concerned with different questions? To what extent may they legitimately give different answers?
3 What difference can it make to the problem of suffering to say that God himself has suffered?
4 For a theology after Auschwitz is it important to be able to say that God himself had an Auschwitz-type experience? Or may a Christian not presume to speak thus on behalf of an essentially Jewish experience?
5 How should Christianity respond to the Holocaust in the light of the history of its treatment of the Jews? A theology of suffering? Silence? Support for the state of Israel?
6 Offer an assessment of Jewish responses to the Holocaust. Is its lesson the pursuit of power or the acceptance of martyrdom?

2 The Buddha and Kierkegaard on suffering: Two religions compared

2.1 The Buddha, suffering and enlightenment

The Four Holy Truths, quoted in Edward Conze, *Buddhism: Its Essence and Development*, Oxford, Oxford University Press, 1974 (1951 edition), p. 43

1. What then is the Holy Truth of Ill [*dukkha*]? Birth is ill, decay is ill, sickness is ill, death is ill. To be conjoined with what one dislikes means suffering [*dukkha*]. To be disjoined from what one likes means suffering. Not to get what one wants, also means suffering . . .
2. What then is the Holy Truth of the Origination of Ill? It is that craving which leads to rebirth, accompanied by delight and greed, seeking its delight now here, now there, i.e. craving for sensuous experience, craving to perpetuate oneself, craving for extinction.
3. What then is the Holy Truth of the Stopping of Ill? It is the complete stopping of that craving, the withdrawal from it, the renouncing of it, throwing it back, liberation from it, non-attachment to it.
4. What then is the Holy Truth of the steps which lead to the stopping of Ill? It is this holy eight-fold Path, which consists of: Right views, right intentions, right speech, right conduct, right livelihood, right effort, right mindfulness, right concentration.

A. Thyagarajan, 'The Tipitakas', in T. M. P. Mahadevan (ed.), *The Great Scriptures: Papers Presented at the First Seminar of the Union for the Study of the Great Religions (India)*, Madras, The G. S. Press, 1956, pp. 90, 95–9

The Tipitakas are the three collections of the teachings of Lord Buddha and his disciples, in the language of Pali, collected and edited in the three great councils, held in ancient times for the purpose, and preserved and protected in the Theravada Lands up to this day [*the older branch of*

Buddhism, found mainly in south-east Asia – e.g. Sri Lanka, Thailand, Cambodia]; and these sacred writings have . . . throughout the centuries enlightened mankind, taught them the path to Nirvana and . . . helped humanity in its struggle to realise the truth. Tipitaka is a Pali word literally meaning 'three baskets or heaps;' it signifies the traditional method of handing down, from one person to another in an unbroken series, the teachings of Buddha in the three collections.

. . .

Now let us review some of the essential teachings of the Tipitakas. 'Just as the waters of the ocean have got only one taste, the taste of salt, so the teachings of Lord Buddha has only one theme, the subject of liberation and freedom.' Lord Buddha in his first sermon to the five Bhikkus [*monks*] said:

> that by avoiding the two extremes of self-indulgence and sensuality on the one hand and self-mortification and extreme austerity on the other, the Tathagata [*another title for the Buddha*] has found out that middle path, which giveth vision, which giveth knowledge, which tends to peace, higher wisdom, enlightenment and Nibbana [*alternative spelling for Nirvana*]. And what is that 'middle path?' It is this very noble eight-fold path, namely, right view, right aspiration, right speech, right activity, right livelihood, right effort, right mindfulness and right concentration. This is that middle path which gives vision, knowledge, higher wisdom, enlightenment and tends to peace and Nibbana.

The teachings of the Buddha is a way of life, a path to perfection, it is a self-discipline leading to enlightenment. This training is on the ethical plane developing the moral life, leading one to the higher way of thinking, opening of insight, intuition, for the realization of truth. The basis, the ground for this training, is the mind, the human mind. The Dhammapada says:

> Mind is the fore-runner of all states of consciousness. Mind is the chief; and they are mind-made. If with a pure mind one speaks or acts, happiness follows the individual close, like the never-departing shadow.

The urge to follow the middle path, the eight-fold path, lies in the understanding, appreciation and experience of life in this world, as being filled with suffering, sorrow and misery in the main.

> Birth is suffering. Decay is suffering, disease is suffering, death is suffering. To be conjoined with things, which we dislike, is suffering. To be separated from things, which we like, is suffering. Not to get what one wants – that also is suffering. In short, these five aggregates, which are the objects of grasping, clinging to, desiring is suffering.
> And there is a cause for this sorrow, 'Dukka', in human life.
> 'Tanha', or craving is the root cause.
> It is the craving that leads back to birth, along with the lure and the lust that finds pleasure, now here, now there, namely the craving for personal pleasure, the craving to be born again, the craving for annihilation.

Conquest of Dukka can occur by getting rid of the root cause of Dukka, namely, craving. The way of destroying craving being the eight-fold path, one has to follow diligently the training of oneself.

. . .

The earnest follower of the teachings of the Master cannot take in anything on trust, on faith, believe a thing without himself experimenting and experiencing. Has not the Master told in the *Kalama Sutta*:

> Do not accept views from hearsay, from tradition, from what has been told, because it is mentioned in the scriptures; do not accept things as truth, because of reason of logic, by inference as being plausible, and because it agrees with one's speculations; do not accept because of the possibility and because the person who told the views is venerable.
> But when you realize, by yourself, that the views are good, faultless, praised by the wise and when carried out and observed and practised in life, lead to good and happiness to you and to others, then only you should accept and abide in them after acquiring them.

. . .

Moral living with meditation, and contemplation for the attainment of Nibbana, are the path to wisdom. Many methods of meditation are mentioned in the Tipitakas ... Of these meditations the practice of the four Brahma Viharas is highly esteemed. They are the practice of Metta or love, compassion, equanimity and bliss.

By these practices the disciple gradually gets rid of the six hindrances, sensual passion, hatred, worry, doubt, sloth and torpor and ignorance, and the four *asavas* which are

> Kāma or sense desire,
> Bhava, the craving to live,
> Dittihi – false view and
> Ajjiva, the mental darkness.

Thus freed, he grows in the knowledge of what Lord Buddha describes in the Anatta Laksana Sutta thus: –

As respects all forms, sensations, perceptions, predispositions, consciousness whatsoever; past, future and present, be it subjective or existing outside; gross or subtle; mean or exalted, far or near, the correct view, in the light of the highest knowledge is as follows: 'This is not mine, this I am not; this is not my ego.'

Perceiving this, the learned and noble disciple conceives an aversion for form, an aversion for sensation, perception, predispositions and consciousness. And in conceiving this aversion, he is divested of passion and by the absence of passion, he becomes free; and when he is free, he becomes aware that he is free and he knows that rebirth is exhausted, that he has lived the holy life and that he has done what is behoved him to do and that he is no more for this world.

And at this stage, the realization of what the Anguttara Nikaya describes is attained by the earnest disciple. He discovers by himself that

it remains a fact and the fixed and necessary constitution of being that all its constituents are transitory; that all its constituents are misery, and that all its elements are lacking in an enduring principle or ego.

Thus being free of the *asavas* of ignorance, passion and hatred, the disciple is completely emancipated from ideas of self and ego and he is filled with compassion for all living things. He becomes an Arahant [*someone who has achieved the Buddhist goal – more commonly spelt Arahat*]:

> Tranquil is the thought, tranquil, the word and deed of him who, rightly knowing, is wholly freed, perfectly peaceful and equipoised.
>
> He is not credulous, he knows the unmade, has severed all ties, and he has put an end to the occasion of good and evil, and has got out wholly all desires.
>
> Called by the wise a Muni [*a sage*], he wanders alone and he is not disturbed by praise or insult.

Brian Hebblethwaite, *Evil, Suffering and Religion*, London, SPCK, 1976, pp. 1–4, 7–8

The story is told of the Buddha that, as the prince Siddhartha Gautama, he was kept by his father the King in the upper rooms of the palace, so that he should never see anything that could upset him. There he was entertained by music and dancing and the sweet delights of women's company. But the women told him of the pleasant groves in the countryside near the city, and Gautama determined to go outside the palace to see them for himself. The King allowed such excursions, giving orders, however, that all those with any kind of affliction should be kept away from the prince's route. Notwithstanding these instructions, Gautama met on his excursions first an old man, then a man with a diseased body, and thirdly a corpse. Thus the prince became acquainted with the facts of senility, disease and death, and was awakened to the impermanence of everything in this world. He was filled with dismay and anxiety; he became disillusioned with the pleasures of the senses, and resolved to abandon them. He left the palace and, overcome with grief for the suffering and passing away of all living beings, withdrew even from his companions, assumed the life of an ascetic and went in search of truth. After several years he abandoned extreme asceticism as a false path, and at length, while meditating beneath a tree, achieved supreme enlightenment. This involved a mental struggle with Mara, the evil one, the Lord of this world of passion, and the realization, through meditation and concentration, of the tranquillity and joy which come when all craving for permanence ceases. In this state of detachment he lost all pride and contempt for others, all self-intoxication. 'My mind was emancipated, ignorance was dispelled, knowledge arose; darkness was dispelled, light arose.'

The story of the Buddha's enlightenment was greatly expanded in later tradition, but from it stem the basic teachings of early Buddhism, and especially the 'Four Supreme (or Noble) Truths': that life is suffering, that suffering is due to craving or desire, that this craving can be eliminated, and that there is a methodical way to such elimination. That way is the 'Supreme (or Noble) Eightfold Path', whose details need not concern us here, except to say that it too reflects the Buddha's own path to enlightenment and tranquillity through meditation and concentration.

Religious experience takes many different forms, and the religions of the world teach many different attitudes to the facts of suffering and evil. But it is not simply a matter of different practical and theoretical responses; the whole problem is seen differently in different religious contexts. We begin this study with the story of the Buddha's path to enlightenment, because early Buddhism stands at one extreme in the spectrum of religious attitudes to suffering, both in the way it sees the problem and in its response.

These two features are brought out very clearly in the story of the Buddha's encounters with the old man, the diseased man and the corpse, and the consequences of those encounters.

In the first place the stress is on suffering rather than on wickedness. What upsets Gautama's peace of mind is the fact of suffering, primarily physical suffering, although his own mental anguish is part of the problem too.

...

The two questions 'why are men often so wicked?' and 'why is there so much suffering in the world?' are certainly perplexing questions. They are different questions, but for us, I suspect, equally pressing ones.

The Buddha was clearly more perplexed by the second question than the first. It was the suffering (not only of men, but of all living beings) that caused his mental anguish in the first place, and became the main theme of his diagnosis of the human situation. It is true that in the struggle with the tempter, Mara, he had to overcome the lure of pride and discontent; and it is true that the Buddha came to believe that the cause of all suffering lay in craving or desire. But this is different from agonizing over human wickedness. To the Buddha the problem was the all-pervasiveness of physical and mental pain.

In the second place, the Buddha's response to suffering was much more a practical response, a way of coping with the facts, than a theoretical attempt to explain or justify the presence of so much suffering in the world. When *we* ask 'why is there so much suffering in the world?', we tend to be looking for a reason, a purpose behind it all. Somehow things must make sense, or lead to something which makes it all worthwhile. But there is none of this in the Buddha's approach to the problem. Admittedly he offers one kind of explanation – a causal explanation in terms of universal craving; but that only pushes the question one stage further back: why are things like that? Why is there so much craving in the world? Why are men so ignorant of the truth, and why should the world be structured in such a way as to foster so much ignorance and suffering? Those questions did not interest the Buddha.

. . .

[I]t is clear that the centrality of belief in God makes a big difference to how the problem strikes people. It is a remarkable feature of early Buddhism that it contains no belief in a supreme Being. One might think that for this reason alone early Buddhism hardly counts as a religion. On the other hand it has many other characteristic features of religion. It offers an all-embracing diagnosis of the human condition, and a way out of the human predicament. It teaches meditative techniques for achieving ultimate release from self and suffering. Above all it holds there to be a final state of enlightenment and release which it calls Nirvana and which it teaches men to think of as their ultimate concern. Furthermore, it organizes itself as a religion, with monks and missionaries and rituals. Any definition of religion which excluded early Buddhism would be too narrow. It should be thought of rather as the classical example of a non-theistic religion (that is, a religion without God).

The case of early Buddhism suggests the following general reflection: the less central belief in God is to a religion, the less will the problem of evil take the form of a demand for explanation. It will rather be a matter of correct diagnosis and the recommendation of a practical way out of the human predicament. Its emphasis will be on coping with the facts of evil. The understanding plays a part, obviously. One has to get the diagnosis right. One has to dispel the illusions of the King's palace where the young Gautama was at first kept shut in by his father. One has to face the facts. But once the facts are faced and the diagnosis made, the real emphasis lies on the best way to cope with and overcome the universal facts of suffering.

2.2 On not explaining

E. A. Burtt (ed.), *The Teachings of the Compassionate Buddha*, New York, Mentor, 1955, pp. 32–6

What was Buddha's position on metaphysical questions? Western students have generally believed that it was a form of agnosticism, since it has some similarities with that viewpoint which is familiar to them. But it should more properly be described as an avoidance of commitment to any of the alternative doctrines on these matters. And his radically practical reason for such avoidance is brought out in many passages, especially in the following selection from Sutta 63 of the Majjhima-Nikaya.

Thus have I heard.

On a certain occasion the Blessed One was dwelling at Savatthi in Jetavana monastery in Anathapindika's Park. Now it happened to the venerable Malunkyaputta, being in seclusion and plunged in meditation, that a consideration presented itself to his mind, as follows:

These theories which the Blessed One has left unexplained, has set aside and rejected – that the world is eternal, that the world is not eternal, that the world is finite, that the world is infinite, that the soul and the body are identical, that the soul is one thing and the body another, that the saint exists after death, that the saint does not exist after death, that the saint both exists and does not exist after death, that the saint neither exists nor does not exist after death – these the Blessed One does not explain to me. And the fact that the Blessed One does not explain them to me does not please me nor suit me. Therefore I will draw near to the Blessed One and inquire of him concerning this matter. If the Blessed One will explain to me, either that the world is eternal, or that the world is not eternal, or that the world is finite, or that the world is infinite, or that the soul and the body are identical, or that the soul is one thing and the body another, or that the saint exists after death, or that the saint does not exist after death, or that the saint both exists and does not exist after death, or that the saint neither exists nor does not exist after death, in that case will I lead the religious life under the Blessed One. If the Blessed One will not explain to me, either that the world is eternal, or that the world is not eternal . . . or that the saint neither exists nor does not exist after death, in that case I will abandon religious training and return to the lower life of a layman.

Then the venerable Malunkyaputta arose at eventide from his seclusion, and drew near to where the Blessed One was; and having drawn near and greeted the Blessed One, he sat down respectfully at one side.

And seated respectfully at one side, the venerable Malunkyaputta spoke to the Blessed One as follows:

. . .

'If the Blessed One knows that the world is eternal, let the Blessed One explain to me that the world is eternal; if the Blessed One knows that the world is not eternal, let the Blessed One explain to me that the world is not eternal. If the Blessed One does not know either that the world is eternal or that the world is not eternal, the only upright thing for one who does not know, or who has not that insight, is to say, "I do not know; I have not that insight."'

. . .

'Pray, Malunkyaputta, did I ever say to you, "Come, Malunkyaputta, lead the religious life under me, and I will explain to you either that the world is eternal, or that the world is not eternal . . . or that the saint neither exists or does not exist after death"?'

'Nay, verily, Reverend Sir.'

'Or did you ever say to me, "Reverend Sir, I will lead the religious life under the Blessed One, on condition that the Blessed One explain to me either that the world is eternal, or that the world is not eternal . . . or that the saint neither exists nor does not exist after death?"'

'Nay, verily, Reverend Sir.'

'So you acknowledge, Malunkyaputta, that I have not said to you, "Come, Malunkyaputta, lead the religious life under me and I will explain to you either that the world is eternal, or that the world is not eternal . . . or that the saint neither exists nor does not exist after death"; and again that you have not said to me, "Reverend Sir, I will lead the religious life under the Blessed One, on condition that the Blessed One explain to me either that the world is eternal, or that the world is not eternal . . . or that the saint neither exists nor does not exist after death." That being the case, vain man, whom are you so angrily denouncing?'

'Malunkyaputta, any one who should say, "I will not lead the religious life under the Blessed One until the Blessed One shall explain to me either that the world is eternal, or that the world is not eternal . . . or that the saint neither exists nor does not exist after death"; – that person would die, Malunkyaputta, before the Tathagata had ever explained this to him.'

'It is as if, Malunkyaputta, a man had been wounded by an arrow thickly smeared with poison, and his friends and companions, his relatives and kinsfolk, were to procure for him a physician or surgeon; and the sick man were to say, "I will not have this arrow taken out until I have learnt whether the man who wounded me belonged to the warrior caste, or to the Brahmin caste, or to the agricultural caste, or to the menial caste."'

'Or again he were to say, "I will not have this arrow taken out until I have learnt the name of the man who wounded me, and to what clan he belongs."'

'Or again he were to say, "I will not have this arrow taken out until I have learnt whether the man who wounded me was tall, or short, or of the middle height."'

'Or again he were to say, "I will not have this arrow taken out until I have learnt whether the man who wounded me was black, or dusky or of a yellow skin."'

'Or again he were to say, "I will not have this arrow taken out until I have learnt whether the man who wounded me was from this or that village, or town, or city."'

. . .

'Accordingly, Malunkyaput, bear always in mind what it is that I have not explained, and what it is that I have explained. And what, Malunkyaputta, have I not explained? I have not explained, Malunkyaputta, that the world is eternal; I have not explained that the world is not eternal; I have not explained that the world is finite; I have not explained that the world is infinite; I have not explained that the soul and the body are identical; I have not explained that the soul is one thing and the body another; I have not explained that the saint exists after death; I have not explained that the saint does not exist after death; I have not explained that the saint both exists and does not exist after death; I have not explained that the saint neither exists nor does not exist after death. And why, Malunkyaputta, have I not explained this? Because, Malunkyaputta, this profits not, nor has to do with the fundamentals of religion, nor tends to aversion, absence of passion, cessation, quiescence, the supernatural faculties, supreme wisdom, and Nirvana; therefore have I not explained it?'

'And what, Malunkyaputta, have I explained? Misery, Malunkyaputta, have I explained; the origin of misery have I explained; the cessation of misery have I explained; and the path leading to the cessation of misery have I explained. And why, Malunkyaputta, have I explained this? Because, Malunkyaputta, this does profit, has to do with the fundamentals of religion, and tends to aversion, absence of passion, cessation, quiescence, knowledge, supreme wisdom, and Nirvana; therefore have I explained it. Accordingly, Malunkyaputta, bear always in mind what it is that I have not explained, and what it is that I have explained.'

2.3 On direct experience

John Snelling, *The Buddhist Handbook: A Complete Guide to Buddhist Teaching, Practice, History and Schools,* **London, Rider, 1987, pp. 3–5**

Buddhism does not demand that anyone accepts its teachings on trust. The practitioner is instead invited to try them out, to experiment with them. If he finds that they work in practice, then by all means he can take them on board. But there is no compulsion; and if he happens to find the truth elsewhere or otherwise, all well and good. This essential freedom from dogma is enshrined in the Buddha's words to the Kālāmas, a people who lived in the vicinity of the town of Kesaputta:

> Come, Kālāmas, do not be satisfied with hearsay or with tradition or with legendary lore or with what has come down in your scriptures or with conjecture or with logical inference or with weighing evidence or with liking for a view after pondering it over or with someone else's ability or with the thought 'The monk is our teacher' *When you know in yourselves* 'These ideas are unprofitable, liable to censure, condemned by the wise, being adopted and put into effect they lead to harm and suffering', then you should abandon them . . . (And conversely:) *When you know in yourselves* 'These things are profitable . . .' then you should practise them and abide in them . . .
>
> . . .

If the Buddhist emphasis is on finding out for oneself, this necessarily places primary emphasis upon *direct religious experience*, as opposed to belief or blind faith. However, one doesn't in the normal course of events just receive deep religious experience as manna from above. Though that can of course happen, one generally has to make a conscious effort. So Buddhism does not so much offer *things to believe* as *things to do*: a vast array of spiritual practices, ranging from moral precepts that one can apply in one's everyday life and virtues that one can cultivate, to meditative practices (a profusion of these) which help to develop untapped spiritual resources: faculties like profound wisdom or clear-seeing and an all-embracing, selfless compassion. Put in Western terms, the ultimate aim of Buddhist practice is to engineer mystical experience: to penetrate the great mystery at the heart of life and find the answers to the knotty problems that have perennially engaged the most developed minds of the human race. This implies a complete spiritual transformation of the person as well.

2.4 Nirvana

John Bowker, *Problems of Suffering in Religions of the World*, Cambridge, Cambridge University Press, 1970, pp. 252–4

Nirvana is certainly not 'heaven' – that is, it is not the relationship of an eternal soul with its creator. It is even inaccurate to talk of 'entering' *nirvana* after death, as though *nirvana* were a literal or metaphorical place. The word used to describe those who have realised *nirvana* is *parinibbuto*, which means 'completely extinct' or 'totally blown out', in the sense that there is no further 'again-becoming' – 'the steadfast go out (*nibbanti*) like this lamp'.

From that it will be clear that it is easier to talk of *nirvana* in negative terms than to give it a positive description:

A wanderer who ate rose-apples spoke thus to the venerable Sariputta:
 'Reverend Sariputta, it is said: "Nirvana, Nirvana." Now, what, your reverence, is Nirvana?'
 'Whatever, your reverence, is the extinction of passion, of aversion, of confusion, this is called Nirvana.'
 'Is there a way, your reverence, is there a course for the realisation of this Nirvana?'
 'There is.'

Sariputta's reply, explaining the way to the realisation of *nirvana*, belongs to the Fourth Truth, 'the way to cessation of *dukkha*'. In connection with the Third Truth, it underlines the extent to which the Buddha and his disciples were unwilling to describe *nirvana*, but preferred to talk about the way leading to it. If it has to be described, it is best done in terms of cessation:

The King said: 'Revered Nagasena, is stopping *nibbana*?
 'Yes sire, stopping is *nibbana*.'
 'How, revered sir, is stopping *nibbana*?'
 'All those foolish average men, sire, who rejoice in the inner and

outer sense-fields, approve of them and cleave to them – they are carried away by that stream, they are not utterly free from birth, old age and dying, from grief, sorrow, suffering, lamentation and despair, they are not, I say, utterly free from anguish. But, sire, the instructed disciple of the ariyans does not rejoice in the inner and outer sense-fields, does not approve of them or cleave to them. For him, not rejoicing in them, not approving of them or cleaving to them craving is stopped; from the stopping of craving is the stopping of grasping; from the stopping of grasping is the stopping of (karmic) becoming; from the stopping of (karmic) becoming is the stopping of birth; from the stopping of birth, old age and dying, grief, sorrow, suffering, lamentation and despair are stopped. Thus is the stopping of this whole mass of anguish. In this way, sire, stopping is *nibbana*.'

But although it is easier to talk of *nirvana* in terms of what it is *not*, it by no means follows that *nirvana* is annihilation. On the contrary, the Buddha rejected the two extremes of annihilation and eternal *atman* [*soul*], and realised *nirvana* as a middle term between the two:

A monk whose mind is thus released cannot be followed and tracked out even by the gods, including Indra, Brahma, and Prajapati, so that they could say, 'There rests the consciousness of a released person.' And why? Even in this actual life, monks, I say that a released person is not to be thoroughly known. Though I thus say and thus preach, some ascetics and brahmins accuse me wrongly, baselessly, falsely and groundlessly, saying that the ascetic Gotama is a nihilist, and preaches the annihilation, destruction and non-existence of an existent being. That is what I am and do not affirm. Both previously and now I preach pain and the cessation of pain.

Pain and the cessation of pain are *both* realisable experiences. *Nirvana* is not even a 'future' state. It can be realised here and now. Precisely because it is cessation of suffering it is easier to describe it in negative terms – in terms of what it has left behind – but the state of cessation is itself so blissful that it does receive positive descriptions as well. Thus Bh. Sangharakshita has summarised some of the most important negative terms: uninterrupted, uncreate, infinite, inextinguishable, cessation of suffering, freedom from longing, uncompounded, farther shore, the beyond, deliverance, extinction, indiscernible, unoppressed, the absolute, unendangered, unattached, deathless, release, liberation, final deliverance, dispassionate, stillness, purity, allayment. But equally Rhys Davids collected some of the most important positive descriptions: the harbour of refuge, the cool cave, the island amidst the floods, the place of bliss, emancipation, liberation, safety, the supreme, the transcendental, the uncreated, the tranquil, the home of ease, the calm, the end of suffering, the medicine for all evil, the unshaken, the ambrosia, the immaterial, the imperishable, the abiding, the further shore, the unending, the bliss of effort, the supreme joy, the ineffable, the detachment, the holy city.

But it is immediately apparent that some of the terms in the two lists coincide, and that they can be either negative or positive depending on the standpoint of the observer. The truth is that *nirvana* lies beyond 'negative' and 'positive': it lies beyond description. It simply *is*, the state in which *dukkha* has ceased.

2.5 Compassion and sacrifice

Letter from the Buddhist Thich Nhat Hanh to Martin Luther King, from his book *Vietnam: The Lotus in the Sea of Fire*, London, SCM, 1967, pp. 117–19

The self-burning of Vietnamese Buddhist monks in 1963 is somehow difficult for the Western Christian conscience to understand. The Press spoke then of suicide, but in the essence, it is not. It is not even a protest. What the monks said in the letters they left before burning themselves aimed only at alarming, at moving the hearts of the oppressors and at calling the attention of the world to the suffering endured then by the Vietnamese. To burn oneself by fire is to prove that what one is saying is of the utmost importance. There is nothing more painful than burning oneself. To say something while experiencing this kind of pain is to say it with utmost courage, frankness, determination and sincerity. During the ceremony of ordination, as practised in the Mahayana tradition [*the major branch of Buddhism, now larger than the earlier Theravada*], the monk candidate is required to burn one, or more, small spots on his body in taking the vow to observe the 250 rules of a bhikshu, to live the life of a monk, to attain enlightenment and to devote his life to the salvation of all beings. One can, of course, say these things while sitting in a comfortable armchair; but when the words are uttered while kneeling before the community of sangha and experiencing this kind of pain, they will express all the seriousness of one's heart and mind, and carry much greater weight.

The Vietnamese monk, by burning himself, says with all his strength and determination that he can endure the greatest of sufferings to protect his people. But why does he have to burn himself to death? The difference between burning oneself and burning oneself to death is only a difference in degree, not in nature. A man who burns himself too much must die. The importance is not to take one's life, but to burn. What he really aims at is the expression of his will and determination, not death. In the Buddhist belief, life is not confined to a period of 60 or 80 or 100 years: life is eternal. Life is not confined to this body: life is universal. To express will by burning oneself, therefore, is not to commit an act of destruction but to perform an act of construction, i.e., to suffer and to die for the sake of one's people. This is not suicide. Suicide is an act of self-destruction, having as causes the following: (1) lack of courage to live and to cope with difficulties; (2) defeat by life and loss of all hope; (3) desire for non-existence (*abhaya*).

This self-destruction is considered by Buddhism as one of the most serious crimes. The monk who burns himself has lost neither courage nor hope; nor does he desire non-existence. On the contrary, he is very courageous and hopeful and aspires for something good in the future. He does not think that he is destroying himself; he believes in the good fruition of his act of self-sacrifice for the sake of others. Like the Buddha in one of his former lives – as told in a story of Jataka – who gave himself to a hungry lioness which was about to devour her own cubs, the monk believes he is practising the doctrine of highest compassion by sacrificing himself in order to call the attention of, and to seek help from, the people of the world.

2.6 Self and suffering

Philip A. Mellor, 'Self and Suffering: Deconstruction and Reflexive Definition in Buddhism and Christianity', *Religious Studies*, 27, 1, 1991, pp. 62, 53, 55, 62–3

For the Buddhist the self is as much an impermanent, conditioned construct causing suffering as the body, but for the Christian the self can be defined ever more fully through suffering. In both contexts self and suffering are associated in a particular way: the more we suffer the more we can clearly experience self (the Christian view); or, the more we experience self the more we suffer (the Buddhist view). The increasingly clear 'I-Thou' relationship between the individual and God, which von Balthasar sees as being characteristic of Christian meditation, reinforces the belief that suffering (as a route towards God) necessitates a deeper understanding of self.

. . .

[*Hans Urs von Balthasar writes:*]

> Behind the specificity of the creature, as well as of the I, stands a will, who affirms the creature, this I and You, and confirms it in its special character.

In other words, the specific 'I' and the general goodness of creation are intimately related. Von Balthasar quotes a meditation of the French priest Fenelon to underline this point:

> God gave me this I, so I owe him not merely all that I have, but all that I am . . . Without God I would not exist; neither would I have the I which I could love, nor the love with which I love this I, nor the will which loves it, nor the thought by which I know myself.

. . .

From this, von Balthasar concludes as follows:

> One thing becomes evident in this: for Christians there is no path to God – be this way mystical or of any other sort – which would not bear the imprint of the cross. One hears practically nothing about this in the countless Christian books on Zen meditation . . . The dark nights of the mystics, where they are Christian and genuine, are by no means just anthropological purifications of the depths of the soul in order to have a better share of the divine light, but a sharing in the passion of Christ. Paul 'makes up what is still lacking in the suffering of Christ'. He does not live from this world for the sake of a superworldly God, but he lives in God's initiative for the world – and this initiative is called the cross . . . The highpoint of Jesus' existence on earth is not the light of Mt. Tabor, but the great darkness on the cross and his cry of abandonment. (M. Kehl (ed.), *The Von Balthasar Reader*, Edinburgh, T & T Clark, 1982, pp. 335–6, 342)

. . .

The contrasting responses to the issue of suffering which have been the subject of this discussion are signified in the devotional objects [characteristic] of each religion. The serene, passive face and the relaxed, open posture of the Buddha-image conveys the complete non-attachment the deconstruction of self aims to facilitate. In contrast, the gaunt, agonized face and mutilated body of Christ on the crucifix expresses eloquently the salvific potential of suffering. The extremities of medieval asceticism, however distasteful they may appear to the modern mind, are clearly one form of exploration of this characteristically Christian paradigm. Thus, the methods of the deconstruction and reflexive definition of self which are characteristic of Buddhism and Christianity respectively are perhaps indicative of a more general divergence between these two religions on the problems of suffering and the religious meaning we can find in the world. In both religions attitudes to self and suffering are related, but the form this relationship takes differs significantly in each context.

2.7 Kierkegaard on truth, Job and Christ

Søren Kierkegaard, *Eighteen Upbuilding Discourses*, ed. H. V. Hong and E. H. Hong, ET Princeton, New Jersey, Princeton University Press, 1990, pp. 233–4, 109–11

There is a truth, the greatness and the grandeur of which we are accustomed to praise by saying admiringly that it is *indifferent* (*ligegyldig*), equally valid (*lige gyldig*), whether anyone accepts it or not; indifferent to the individual's particular condition, whether he is young or old, happy or dejected; indifferent to its relation to him, whether it benefits him or harms him, whether it keeps him from something or assists him to it; equally valid whether he totally subscribes to it or coldly uses it for ill gain; indifferent to whether he has found it himself or merely repeats what has been taught. And the only one whose understanding was sound and whose admiration was justified was the one who grasped the greatness of this indifference and in accord with it let himself be formed into an indifference toward what pertained to him or any other human being as a human being or especially as a human being.

There is another kind of truth or, if this is humbler, another kind of truths that could be called *concerned truths*. They do not live on a lofty plane, for the simple reason that, ashamed, as it were, they are conscious of not applying universally to all occasions but only specifically to particular occasions. They are not indifferent to the single individual's particular condition, whether he is young or old, happy or defected, because this determines for them whether they are to be truths for him. Neither do they promptly let go of the individual and forsake him, but they continue to be concerned about him until he himself completely breaks away, and even to this they are not indifferent, although he is not able to make these truths doubtful about themselves. Such a truth is not indifferent to how the individual receives it, whether he wholeheartedly appropriates it or it becomes mere words to him. This very difference certainly shows that it is jealous of itself, is not indifferent to whether the truth becomes a blessing or a ruination to him, since this contrary decision witnesses specifically against the equal validity; it is not indifferent to whether he honestly places his confidence in it or whether, himself deceived, he wants to deceive others, since this avenging wrath expressly shows that it is not indifferent. Such a concerned truth is not independent of the one who has propounded it; on the contrary, he remains present in it continually in order in turn to concern himself about the single individual.

. . .

> Then Job arose, and tore his robe, and shaved his head, and fell upon the ground, and worshiped, saying: Naked I came from my mother's womb, and naked shall I return; the Lord gave, and the Lord took away; blessed be the name of the Lord.
> (Job 1:20–21)

Not only do we call someone a teacher of humankind who by a special stroke of fortune discovered some truth or fathomed it by unflagging toil and thoroughgoing persistence and then left his attainment as learning that subsequent generations strive to understand and in this understanding to appropriate to themselves; but we also call someone – perhaps in an even stricter sense – a teacher of humankind who had no teaching to hand over to others but left humankind only himself as a prototype, his life as a guide for everyone, his name as security for many, his work as an encouragement for those who are being tried.

Such a teacher and guide of humankind is Job, whose significance by no means consists in what he said but in what he did. He did indeed leave a statement that by its brevity and beauty has become a proverb preserved from generation to generation, and no one has presumptuously added anything to it or taken anything from it; but the statement itself is not the guide, and Job's significance consists not in his having said it but in his having acted upon it. The saying itself is certainly beautiful and worth pondering, but if someone else had said it, or if Job had been someone else, or if he had said it on another occasion, the saying itself would also have become something different – meaningful, if it had any meaning at all, as spoken, but not meaningful because he acted by asserting it, because the asserting was itself an action. If Job had applied his whole life to an inculcation of this saying, if he had regarded it as the sum and substance of what a person ought to let life teach him, if he had merely kept on *teaching* it but had never attempted it himself, had himself never acted in his asserting it, then Job would have been someone different and his significance would have been different. Then Job's name would have been forgotten, or at least it would not have mattered whether anyone knew it – the important point would be the contents of the words, the richness of the thought that lay in them. If humankind had received this saying, then it would have been this that one generation passed on to the next, whereas now it is Job himself who accompanies the generation. When one generation has finished its service, completed its work, fought through its struggle, Job has accompanied it; when the new generation with its incalculable ranks, each individual in his place, stands ready to begin the pilgrimage, Job is there again, takes his place, which is the outpost of humanity. If the generation sees nothing but happy days in prosperous times, then Job faithfully accompanies it; but if the single individual experiences the terror in thought, is anguished over the thought of what horror and distress life can have in store, over the thought that no one knows when the hour of despair may strike for him, then his troubled thought seeks out Job, rests in him, is calmed by him, for Job faithfully accompanies him and comforts him, not, to be sure, as if he had suffered once and for all what would never be suffered again, but comforts as someone who witnesses that the horror has been suffered, the horror has been experienced, the battle of despair has been fought to the glory of God, for his own rescue, for the benefit and joy of others. In happy days, in prosperous times, Job walks along at the generation's side and safeguards its happiness, grapples with the anxious dream that some sudden unspeakable horror will assail a person and have the power to murder his soul as its certain prey. Only a light-minded person could wish that Job were not along, that his revered name did not remind him of what he is trying to forget, that life also has terror and anxiety; only a selfish person could wish that Job did not exist so that the idea of his suffering would not disturb his flimsy happiness with its rigorous earnestness and scare him out of a sense of security drunk with callousness and damnation. In tempestuous times, when the foundation of existence is tottering, when the moment shivers in anxious expectancy of what may come, when every explanation falls silent at the spectacle of the wild tumult, when a person's innermost being groans in despair and 'in bitterness of soul' cries to heaven, then Job still walks along at the generation's side and guarantees that there is a victory, guarantees that even if the single individual loses in the struggle, there is still a God who, just as he proportions every temptation humanly, even though a person did not withstand the temptation, will still make its outcome so that we are able to bear it – yes, even more gloriously than any human expectancy. Only the defiant person could wish that Job did not exist, that he could completely divest his soul of the last love still present in the wail of despair, that he could whine about life, indeed, curse life in such a way that there would not be even an echo of faith and trust and humility in his words, that in his defiance he could stifle the scream in order not to create the impression that there was anyone whom it provoked. Only a soft person could wish that Job did not exist, that he could instead leave off thinking, the sooner the better, could give up all movement in the most disgusting powerlessness, could blot himself out in the most wretched and miserable forgetfulness.

Søren Kierkegaard, *Gospel of Sufferings*, ET Cambridge, James Clarke, 1955, pp. 30–1

It was by no means Christ's intention to lead men out of the world to realms of Paradise where was neither want nor misery, or as by a magician's wand to transform our life on earth into worldly joy and happiness. This was only a misconception of the Jews, superficial and frivolous. But he would teach, what he demonstrated by his example, how the burden is light even when the suffering is heavy. And so in one sense the burden remains the same, for the burden is just the suffering, the heavy suffering, and yet this burden has become light. Because Christianity has come into the world, man's lot has not thereby become another earthly lot than it was before. A Christian may have to suffer exactly as he suffered before, but yet for a Christian the heavy burden has become light. This, first, we shall ponder; and afterwards more especially consider what is the light burden the Christian in particular must bear.

When we talk about bearing burdens in the language of every day, we distinguish between a light burden and a heavy one; we say it is easy to bear the light burden, hard to bear the heavy one. But we are not speaking of this now; we speak of the far more solemn theme, that one and the same burden should be heavy and yet light; we speak of a miracle and a wonder – for is it any greater wonder to turn water into wine, than that a heavy burden should continue to be heavy and yet be light? And yet there are occasions when we do speak like this also. When a man, for instance, is at the point of sinking under the heavy burden he bears, but that burden is his dearest possession, then he says that it is a light burden. Such things are seen in the world. We look with horror on the miser who drags himself along under the killing weight of his treasure, yet counts this heavy burden light, because his treasure is his all. We contemplate in silent exaltation of spirit a man bearing what in a good sense is for him the most precious thing in the world, finding it truly heavy, and yet light. When one who loves is in distress in the sea, and at the point of drowning because of the weight of her whom he loves and whom he wants to save, then his burden is certainly heavy, and yet – yes, ask him! – yet so unspeakably light. Though there be two of them in danger of life, and the other pull him down, yet has he but one desire, to save his life; and so he is speaking as if the burden did not even exist, calling her his life, and he would save his life. How does this change come about? Is it not perhaps through a thought, an idea, that intervenes? The burden is heavy, he says. But now the thought or the idea interposes, and he says: Nay, ah nay, but how light it is! Is he then insincere because he speaks thus? Not at all; when he speaks truly thus, then he truly loves. And so it is by the power of the thought, of the idea, of love, that the change is brought about.

2.8 Some explanatory notes on Buddhism

David Webster

From China to California, Buddhist monasteries continue a way of life instituted over two thousand years ago. From Hawaii to Hull, people stop by to spend a calm hour at meditation classes after work. Buddhism is a global religion; but while most of us know *of* Buddhism, many feel that they do not know *about* Buddhism. The image of the shaven-headed monk begging for food on their alms-round is familiar and evocative, but what do Buddhists actually believe?

Buddhism contains a huge diversity, both within its practice and its doctrinal belief. From its inception, Buddhism has been a religion seriously concerned with the refining and clarification of its teachings. One consequence of this is that it is a religion which is as doctrinally fragmented as Christianity. Given this, and to maintain a sense of perspective, we should perhaps begin at the beginning with the historical Buddha.

The dates for the life of the Buddha (the 'Awakened One') vary, depending on which sources you examine, but something in the region of 448–368 BC seems likely, and virtually all agree on his life-span of eighty years. Born in north-east India (in a region that now straddles the border with Nepal), and with the given name of Siddhattha Gotama (sometimes written Siddhartha Gautama), incredible stories surround the birth of the Buddha. He is said to have walked and spoken immediately after his birth, proclaiming that this was to be his 'last birth' (as we shall see, Buddhists believe that we have all had many previous lives).

Gotama's life can be split into three key periods. The first is the period of his upbringing and early adulthood and marriage. The second stage begins when he renounced all this for the life of a religious seeker after truth. This phase was completed by his 'enlightenment', and can be seen as the beginning of Buddhism. This continues to his death, by which time the Buddhist tradition was a thriving competitor in the crowded and lively religious context of the time. The early life of Gotama was one of relative luxury, whereas the second period was often characterised by the practice of harsh asceticism (towards the end of this phase, Gotama almost died from starving himself in the hope of some spiritual benefit). The enlightenment represents the discovery of a 'middle-way' between these two extremes, and this notion of a middle-way is also found in Buddhist philosophy.

To get a sense of the concerns of Buddhism, of what motivates its practices, we can look at what led the young Gotama to abandon his life of luxury and privilege, and turn to a life of struggle and hardship. According to the traditional accounts, Gotama's mother had a prophetic dream while pregnant, which was interpreted as setting out two possible destinies for her unborn son. He would either become a great worldly leader, a mighty emperor; or he would become a religious teacher. His father, often portrayed as a king – more likely a local clan-leader, preferred the former. To prevent his son developing an interest in religion, the young Gotama is said to have been shielded from knowledge of the world's unpleasant aspects, lest he become interested in spiritual matters. As we know, this strategy failed; but why it failed is revealing. On rides out in his carriage, Gotama witnesses a sick person, an old person and a corpse. After questioning his driver, he is deeply distressed by this knowledge of ageing, sickness and death – facts of life that had been previously kept from him. While still disturbed by these sights, he later witnesses an ascetic, with an appearance of calm, and wishes to find out how someone can be so seemingly happy in such an unsatisfactory world. One night, alone, Gotama slips away and, to use the phrase often found of Buddhist monks and nuns, goes forth from home to homelessness.

What this story tells us is what Gotama was seeking: a way to find happiness in a world of ageing, sickness and death. In the Buddhist view, he eventually finds just this. The answer, the way beyond this world of frustration and suffering, is *Nirvana*. Just what this means is often hard to express, but some things can be said about it. Once a person has attained this goal, they will not be reborn anymore. Normally, death is followed by birth – be it is as a human, an animal, or in some other realm (in a Hell, if we deserve it, or a Heavenly state). For the one who has attained *Nirvana*, this process is at an end. And yet *Nirvana* (despite being, as a word, linked to the notion of being 'extinguished' – as in a flame) is explicitly not seen as a form of annihilation. In practice, few Buddhists worry too much about the goal, preferring to concentrate on the path to the goal.

The Buddhist world-view

In order, however, to make sense of Buddhist teachings, we need to see them in the context of a particular world-view. The world-view that I describe here applies most specifically to early Buddhism (and the only surviving form of early Buddhism – *Theravada* Buddhism, found in Sri Lanka and parts of south-east Asia), but the later schools of thought add to this view, rather than rejecting it.

As we have seen, Buddhism believes we have many lives, stretching innumerably back into the past. But what of key religious issues that we are used to thinking about in the West, such as God and creation? Neither of these is central to Buddhist thought. Creation, so fundamental to Christian thought, is seen as of limited interest to many Buddhists. Indeed, at times the Buddha seems to indicate that questions regarding the origins of the universe are a distraction. To use the analogy found in the texts, asking where the world comes from, or why it is how it is, is like being shot in the eye with an arrow and, rather than asking how to remove the arrow, asking, 'What wood is this made from?', 'Who made this arrow?' Buddhism, then, is concerned with how we react to the world as it is, rather than primarily being a means of explaining how it got to be like this. Buddhism can do this because it does not credit the Buddha, or any omnipotent divine being, with the creation of the world. In fact, Buddhism is sometimes, particularly in its earlier forms, described as being a form of atheism. This requires some qualification.

Buddhism emerged in the context of widespread theistic belief in gods that are associated with the religion we now know as Hinduism. Buddhism did not deny the existence of these beings, indeed the Buddha converses with them at times, and they gather in great numbers to witness the end of his life. What Buddhism does is to alter the status of these *devas* (gods). Rather than being seen as all-knowing, and part of some divine essence, Buddhism sees them as part of the circle of birth, death and rebirth. The gods may be powerful, but not all-powerful. In the Buddhist view, the gods are ignorant (why else would they wish to hear the Buddha teach?), and also subject to death and rebirth (although they have very long life-spans). In this context, there is a sense in which, odd though it may sound, God or gods are almost irrelevant to religion. They have little to teach us, and we must seek our salvation independently of them.

Another key aspect of Buddhist thought is the teaching of 'not-Self' (*anatta*). This is the view that people (and indeed all other beings) are a collection of changing, temporary processes. In this view, there is no aspect of a person (such as a Soul or deep inner Self) which is eternal and unchanging. This is an important teaching, and one which later schools of Buddhist thought expand in a variety of ways.

Buddhist teachings

In order to get a sense of Buddhist teachings, we may turn now to the most common expression of Buddhist doctrine: The Four Noble Truths. These 'Truths' are expounded in the earliest texts of Buddhism, and represent a view of the human condition as well as articulating how we might best respond to this condition.

The first of these truths is 'The Noble Truth of *dukkha*.' This states 'Birth is *dukkha*, ageing is *dukkha*, sickness is *dukkha*, death is *dukkha*; sorrow, lamentation, pain, grief and despair are *dukkha*; association with what one dislikes is *dukkha*, separation from what one likes is *dukkha*, not to get what one wants is *dukkha*; in short the five groups of grasping (those elements which make up a person) are *dukkha*.'

But what is *dukkha*? Although it is often translated as 'suffering', there are various aspects to *dukkha*. In its first sense it is basic biological pain and suffering which we all suffer – the basic pains of birth, life, ageing, sickness and death. Secondly, there is the physical and mental suffering which arises throughout life due to the various problems we encounter. The third category relates to the frustrations of life. We can never fully avoid that which we dislike, or be with that which we do like. We grasp at the things we love, but they always pass away. There is nothing which we can truly rely upon in the long run. A fourth sense of *dukkha* is a general longing for 'something more' from life; a desire to escape the grind and suffering of life. This could be seen as a sense of pervasive disappointment, and some have compared it to the existentialist idea of *angst*.

The causes of *dukkha* are diagnosed by the second Noble Truth (although this analysis relies upon the claim that all worldly phenomena are impermanent). The cause of *dukkha* is tanha – literally thirst. This term is usually rendered as 'craving', and represents the reason we often have to live with so much stress and disappointment.

While this may all be starting to look a little grim, the third Truth is seen as offering a solution to this problem. It suggests that we can end *tanha*, and so end *dukkha*, which is seen as equivalent to attaining the final goal – Nirvana.

The final Noble Truth gives a prescription for how we might move towards the Buddhist goal. The fourth Truth is the 'Eightfold Path' (if you think that Buddhism is rather keen on lists, you are right – Buddhist doctrinal texts are often full of lists of this type). I will not list all eight aspects here, but summarise them in three categories. These are three kinds of behaviour which form the basis of Buddhist life and practice. There are moral injunctions, which require us to live a good life (many of these are stricter for monks and nuns than for lay Buddhists). There are portions of the Path concerned with wisdom, which help us to overcome the ignorance that leads us to harmful actions, as well as assisting us in understanding the teachings. The other key area of the Path, which in many ways integrates the first two, is meditation. While Buddhism does contain devotional and ritual aspects, the most important practice, at least for most schools of Buddhism, is meditation. This is seen as a practical tool whereby we can intervene in our own mental processes, and begin to undermine those factors that lead us to act in ways that cause harm, to our self and to others.

This whirlwind tour of the doctrinal basis of Buddhist thought should indicate that while Buddhism contains no real sense of a problem of 'sin' or 'evil', the reduction (and final cessation) of suffering is what sits at the heart of Buddhist concern and motivation.

Topics for discussion

1 To what extent is talk of 'the problem of suffering' and 'the problem of evil' talk about two different things?
2 What sort of questions did the Buddha believe did not 'tend to edification' and why?
3 What account does the Buddha give of the relation between suffering, desire, consciousness and the self? Does this mean that he did after all engage in metaphysical speculation?
4 What is meant by *nirvana*? In what ways is it similar or dissimilar to the Christian notion of heaven? To what extent is it legitimate to speak of either concept as an 'answer' to the problem of suffering?

5 Explore the Christian and Buddhist understandings of 'self' and the implication this might have for their different evaluations of suffering.
6 In what ways does Kierkegaard believe that 'edifying discourse' or 'concerned truth' might transform a person's attitude to suffering? Does this place him at the opposite pole to the teaching of Buddha, or is some dialogue possible?

3 The varieties of theodicy

3.1 The problem posed

John L. Mackie, *The Miracle of Theism: Arguments For and Against the Existence of God*, Oxford, Oxford University Press, 1982, pp. 150–3

According to traditional theism, there is a god who is both omnipotent (and omniscient) and wholly good, and yet there is evil in the world. How can this be? It is true that there is no explicit contradiction between the statements that there is an omnipotent and wholly good god and that there is evil. But if we add the at least initially plausible premises that good is opposed to evil in such a way that a being who is wholly good eliminates evil as far as he can, and that there are no limits to what an omnipotent being can do, then we do have a contradiction. A wholly good omnipotent being would eliminate evil completely; if there really are evils, then there cannot be any such being.

The problem of evil, in the sense in which I am using this phrase, is essentially a logical problem: it sets the theist the task of clarifying and if possible reconciling the several beliefs which he holds. It is not a scientific problem that might be solved by further discoveries, nor a practical problem that might be solved by a decision or an action. And the problem in this sense signally does not arise for those whose views of the world are markedly different from traditional theism.

. . .

The possibility of a solution lies in the fact that either or both of the additional premises suggested above may be modified: the opposition between good and evil may be construed in such a way that a wholly good god would not, after all, eliminate evil as far as he could, and (whether this is so or not) it may be argued that there are limits – and limits that matter in this context – to what even an omnipotent being can do.

For example, it would usually be said that God cannot do what is logically impossible; and this, we can agree, would be no real departure from omnipotence.

. . .

Popular theodicies, that is, attempts to justify God in the face of the widespread occurrence of what are at the same time held to be evils, make far more use of the notion that evil is often necessary as a means to good. Of course this way of thinking is entirely natural for human agents in the ordinary circumstances of life. It may well be that children can develop into responsible self-governing adults only by being allowed to make mistakes and to learn from them. Parents, teachers, and statesmen, among others, constantly use, or permit, as means to what they see as good, things which, considered on their own, they regret or deplore. Any sensible person may be ready, though he regards pain in itself as an evil, to put up with painful medical treatment if he is convinced that it is necessary as a means to a lasting improvement in his health, or to endure toil that is in itself undesirable for the sake of commensurate rewards. Also, taking a wider view, it is reasonable to say that though pain, as experienced by animals of many kinds, is bad in itself, it performs a useful warning function: it directs the animal away from what would cause greater injury or death. Even pain which does not itself serve this useful purpose is in general causally connected with that which is beneficial: it would be hardly possible for animals to have nervous systems of the sorts that enable them to be guided by pain away from sources of harm without thereby being liable sometimes to suffer pain that, on these particular occasions, brings no good results. Such truths as these are familiar and obvious; but they are also totally irrelevant. For since they all concern causal relationships, in which something counted as evil is seen to be causally necessary as a means to, or as a result or accompaniment of, something that can be seen as a greater, counterbalancing, good, they explain only why agents whose power is limited by independently existing causal laws may reasonably put up with evil for the sake of the associated good. But God, by hypothesis, is not such an agent. If omnipotence means anything at all, it means power over causal laws. If there is an omnipotent creator, then if there are any causal laws he must have made them, and if he is still omnipotent he must be able to override them.

Terence Penelhum, 'Divine Goodness and the Problem of Evil', *Religious Studies*, 2, 1966–7, pp. 95–6

Let us first present the problem of evil in its traditional, logical guise. The argument is that it is inconsistent for anyone to believe both of the following two propositions:

I. The world is the creation of a God who is omnipotent, omniscient, and wholly good.
II. The world contains evil.

Both, especially the first, are highly complex propositions, and it is natural that the problem is often put as one of the apparent inconsistency of holding three or four or more propositions at once. Although the complexity of I is vital, the problem can be stated well enough in this deceptively simple form. Let us begin by recognising two things about the problem as presented. (a) Apart from some eminent and disingenuous theologians, proposition II is not itself a challenge to theism. It is a part of it. The existence of evil is not something the facts of life force the theist to admit, in the way in which the facts of the fossil evidence forced some nineteenth century theists to admit the antiquity of the world. The existence of evil is something the theist emphasises. Theists do not see fewer evils in the world than atheists; they see more. It is a necessary truth that they see more. For example, to the theist adultery is not only an offence against another person or persons, but also an offence against a sacrament, and therefore against God; it is therefore a worse offence, because it is a compound of several offences. Atheists can never be against sin, for to atheists there can be no sins, 'sin' being a theological concept that only has application if God exists. Only if this is accepted can the problem of evil be represented as a logical problem. For a charge of inconsistency can only be levelled against the theist if he holds both of the allegedly inconsistent propositions *as part of his belief*. The nineteenth-century theist who finally accepted the antiquity of the world could not have been accused of logical inconsistency unless a belief like that of the world's beginning in 4004 BC were entailed by his form of theism. (b) Given this, it is easy to see why the logical challenge the problem of evil presents is so serious. For the theist, in believing in God, believes *both* that God created the world *and* that much that is in the world is deeply deficient in the light of the very standards God himself embodies. The inconsistency seems to result from two distinguishable functions which the idea of God has. It is an ultimate source of explanations of why things

3.2 Some solutions offered

Jeff Astley, *God's World*, London, Darton, Longman & Todd, 2000, p. 60, 62–3, 65–6

To call a situation or act evil is to say that in and of itself it is a bad thing (it is 'intrinsically' evil). This is true even if it leads to other good things (when we may say that it is also 'instrumentally' good), or if it is part of a larger good situation . . .

There is no single explanation of evil within the Christian tradition. The following attempts have achieved wide circulation, while remaining contentious . . .

Three responses to the intellectual problem of evil

'SOME PAIN IS INEVITABLE IN ANY UNIVERSE'
Perhaps suffering is, as philosophers would say, 'logically necessary' – inevitable in any possible world. According to Austin Farrer, natural evil is a consequence of the fact that physical objects take up space, so that matter inevitably interacts and collides with other matter. The cancer in the lung and the fungus in the foot cause pain because two things are trying to occupy the same space. 'The mutual interference of systems', Farrer claims, is 'the grand cause of physical evil'; adding that 'the physical universe could be delivered from the mutual interference of its constituent systems only by being deprived of its physicality'. Hence God does not intend earthquakes; they are 'necessary consequences . . . of the order of Nature' (Keith Ward). In order to avoid such suffering, God *could* have created only minds or spirits (for example, angels) that do not occupy space. But if he had restricted his creative urge in this way, God would not have created *us*.

'SUFFERING IS A RESULT OF SIN'
The 'free will defence' argues that it is better that God should have made free, responsible people who *might* do wrong, rather than not allowing free will at all. The doctrine of the Fall is an extension of this claim, and adherents of this doctrine argue that some of the natural evil in the world is a consequence of the sin of Adam or Satan.

'SUFFERING IS NECESSARY IF THE WORLD IS TO BE A PLACE WHERE WE CAN GROW UP MORALLY'

John Hick asks us to imagine a world without pain, and therefore without challenges and problems: 'life would become like a reverie in which, delightfully but aimlessly, we should float and drift at ease'. Is such a world too good to be good-for-us? Don't we want more from life, and for our children, than effortless pleasure? It is only in a world where there are real difficulties, dangers and suffering that we can develop courage and intelligence, and compassion and self-sacrifice. One of the main reasons for creating a world containing suffering is to encourage our battle against evil. To adopt John Keats' phrase, our world should be thought of as a 'vale of soul-making', and emphatically not as a harmless cage for a pampered pet. And is it not also true that it is only those who have suffered who can show us what it is like to be a real human being?

But do all 'first-order evils' give rise to these 'second-order' goods? We might respond to this criticism with an appeal to the mystery of evil, arguing that suffering has to be distributed randomly ('gratuitously') if it is to serve its soul-making function. The reason for this is that if the sufferer's pain was clearly seen to be for her ultimate good (as leading to her moral and spiritual development), or as her just desert, it would neither evoke sympathy and aid nor encourage disinterested virtue.

...

Contrasting theodicies

According to Hick, two contrasting theodicies may be found within the Christian tradition: the 'Augustinian' and the 'Irenaean'. The chart below is constructed from his summary of their points of contrast and agreement (cf. Hick, *Evil and the God of Love*, 1968, Ch. XII).

'AUGUSTINIAN'	**'IRENAEAN'**
(e.g. Augustine, Aquinas, Calvin, Leibniz, and many traditional Catholic and Protestant accounts)	*(e.g. Irenaeus, Schleiermacher, Tennant, and many modern liberal accounts)*
Responsibility for evil rests on created beings (angels and/or human beings) who have misused their freedom. Moral evil is their fault, and natural evil is the	It is explicitly recognised that **God is ultimately responsible for the evil in the universe**. Moral evil is the fault of free human beings that God has created and permits to sin. God

inevitable consequence (punishment) for that moral evil. has deliberately put natural evil in the world to create the best environment for soul-making.

This tradition appeals to certain metaphysical views:
- evil is 'non-being' (God only creates good; evil is a going-wrong of good or is to be found where things are at the limits of existence);
- while some of the parts may be ugly, the whole picture is more beautiful as a result of the contrast;
- 'the principle of plenitude' (it is better for God to create at all the levels of existence, so that the universe is as full as it can be of beings – including those that suffer evil or cause it).

This tradition holds no such metaphysical views.

God's relationship with the universe is impersonal. Humans are created to complete the list of types of being.

God's relationship with the universe is essentially personal. Humans are created for fellowship with God.

Looks to the past (the Fall) for an explanation of the origin of evil.

Looks to the future (heaven) for the justifying end, as God brings good out of evil.

The Fall is central to this theodicy: Adam (Man) was created perfect in a perfect world, but sinned deliberately.

The Fall is less important, or is denied altogether. Some argue that the Fall of Adam was like the sin of a child; others that mankind was created or evolved as 'fallen'. (Down here in the mud of the world, we might say, we are free to grow towards God without being overwhelmed by any direct knowledge of the divine nature.)

The present world is not how God intends it to be. It should be a paradise without suffering, and human beings need to be saved from it by God's grace.	**The world is more-or-less how God intends it**. It is a world with real temptations and risks: the only sort of world in which we can freely develop faith and virtue, and learn obedience through suffering, in co-operation with God's grace.
Our behaviour in this world will determine **our ultimate destination in heaven or hell**.	This tradition is **more likely to reject the notion of hell**. In the end all will be saved, perhaps through a continuing process of soul-making after death.

[*The readings from Hick (the Irenaean) and Farrer (predominantly Augustinian), together with Horne's account of Augustine, may usefully be compared and contrasted to illustrate this analysis.*]

3.3 The principle of plenitude and the screening of God

Austin Farrer, *Love Almighty and Ills Unlimited*, London, Collins, 1962, pp. 64–6, 69–73

We cannot describe our Creator's choice as the act of the God that he is. We can only describe it as the act of a man, with whom we are pleased to compare him. No doubt, if we make such comparisons, we make them for the sake of a moral which we hope to be divine, in spite of the human basis of our analogy. But we cannot be sure that the hope is justified. . . . We, for our part, will make the confession of our folly, and write out a fable or two about the creative choice. Here, then, is the first of them.

The divine Goodness desires the existence of creatures that shall be excellent. Not, however, that shall be of the highest excellence; for the highest belongs to the divine nature alone. God fulfils in himself all that is possible on that supreme level. To realise the divinest good, he has not to create, but to live. But there are lower levels of excellence possible; and it is better they should be filled, than lie empty. A gardener may have filled the best beds he has, where the aspect is fair, and the soil deep. He may still wish to plant other grounds, where much beauty, though not the highest, can be brought to flourish. So God plants over the next best soil available to him; he extends existence to archangels, pure spirits though finite; each a limited mirror of his own perfection, each viewing him from a distinct point of vantage; each answering the vision with a unique obedience. These beds being planted, the divine gardener takes pity on the next best, and after those, on the next best again; and so down through many ranks and hierarchies of angels, as far as the humblest sort of pure spirits. These having been created, a fresh choice has to be made. All the possibility of spiritual nature has been realised – everything you could call garden soil has been brought under cultivation. Only dry walls and rocks remain. What can the gardener do with stones? He can slip little plants into the crannies; and he may reckon it the furthest stretch of his art, to have made such barrenness bloom. So, beyond the spiritual there lies the possibility of the material. The creator does not hold his hand. It is better a physical universe, with its inevitable flaws, should be, than not be; and from the stony soil of matter he raises first living, and then reasonable creatures.

. . .

God's desire was to create beings able to know and to love him. Yet, in the nature of the case, there lay a dilemma. In proportion to their capacity for such love or knowledge, the created minds or wills would be dominated by the object of their knowledge or their love; they would lose the personal initiative which could alone give reality to their knowing or their loving. The divine glory would draw them into itself, as the candle draws the moth. You might say, 'Why should not he shade the light? Could not God put a screen between himself and his creatures?' But of what would the screen consist? A screen, literally understood, is a physical barrier; and it screens a physical object from an organ of physical vision. God is a spirit; and the hypothesis we are examining is of purely spiritual creatures also. What sort of screen could God interpose between himself and them? And where would it stand?

. . .

There cannot, admittedly, be a physical screen in the literal meaning of the term; for a screen must stand between physical senses and their physical objects; and even if God gives his creatures physical senses, he cannot make himself a physical thing. But suppose he creates a whole physical world, and places creaturely minds in it; suppose he so attaches them to it, that they are initially turned towards it, and find in it their natural concern. May he not then have strong animal minds, aspiring to know him in spite of their native physicality, instead of feeble spirits, whose obstacle lies in the mere poverty of their spirituality?

Might we perhaps say that the first requirement is to have a created world which is quite other than God? Then, by identification with such a world, godlike creatures may keep their distinctness from God, and not fall straight back into the lap of creating power. To express the idea, we borrow the pen of an ancient rabbi.

The Holy One (blessed be he!) when he sought to create the first Age, whereunto was he like? Like our father Noah, looking for a second Age, after the first had perished by water. He sent forth birds from him out of the Ark, and twice they returned. He said, 'There is as yet no world in which to plant.' He sent a third time, and the bird returned not. He said, 'Dry ground appears,' and presently, going forth from the Ark, he planted the stock of the vine. So likewise the Holy One, in the meditations of his creative thought, sent forth an archangel; and the archangel returned into the mind that sent him. After him, an angel in like manner; and the angel returned also. He said, 'There is no ground in which they might root themselves.' Then he sent forth a simple thing, without understanding, and so small that no eye but his (blessed be he!) could perceive it. And it returned not, not knowing the way; for in its simplicity it knew not anything. He sent forth another such, and the two clung together; and so another and another, multitudes without number; and they clung to the first. He said 'A firm ground appears,' and he set foot upon it. There caused he to grow up the garden of Eden. Moreover he took the dust of that ground, and moulded our father Adam, shaping him in the image and similitude of God.

. . .

The story has the advantage not only of explaining why God should create at so low a level as the physical, but also of squaring with what we know about the world we live in. For, to all evidence, the world-process begins with the most elementary organisation of energy, and builds gradually up, level by level. So we shall be likely to feel that the Ark-parable is altogether more enlightening than the garden-parable.

3.4 Evil as non-being

Brian Horne, *Imagining Evil*, London, Darton, Longman & Todd, 1996, pp. 38–45

We shall find that when it comes to the question of evil . . . [that] Augustine is often at his most severely abstract, yet here, at the same time, all his imaginings of evil are drenched with the seat of his personal struggle. In Milan, under the guidance of the great bishop Ambrose, Augustine left Neoplatonism for Christianity; but not before he had gathered to himself

. . . certain aspects of that teaching which could never be erased from his thought [*the Neoplatonists were a group of philosophers influenced by the third-century thinker Plotinus*]. One of these was a conception of evil as a kind of nihilism; not a cosmic principle at war with goodness, but a nothingness, 'something' which had fallen away from being.

In the seventh book of the *Confessions* Augustine gives us an account of his search for the answer to the problem of evil in a reconstruction of the movement of his thoughts from the perspective of faith:

> . . . where and whence is evil? How did it creep in? What is its root and what is its seed? Or does it not have any being? Why should we fear and avoid what has no being? If our fear is vain, it is certain that fear itself is evil, and that the heart is groundlessly disturbed and tortured . . . Where then does it come from since the good God made everything good? . . . Is it that the matter from which he made things was somehow evil?

Augustine rejected the Manichean solution that matter could, in itself, be evil [*Manichaeism, an extreme version of Persian dualism, held an absolute distinction between good and evil*]; instead he adopted, from the Neoplatonists, the doctrine that evil could never be considered to be 'substantial', but was a lack, an absence. It could have no real, independent existence; it was not the opposite of good, but the absence of good, a 'nothing' a *privatio boni*. As a Christian Augustine was committed to the assertion that everything that God had created was good, and since God was the Creator of everything, evil could have no real existence, for this would be to suppose another creator. Evil was the absence of good in the same way that sickness was the absence of health and darkness was the absence of light. Does a shadow exist? Not of itself. It is defined by the light which does exists: it comes into 'being' and can be observed and experienced only as a result of the withdrawal of the light. The seductive propositions of dualism were that everything can be known by its direct and complementary opposite; that the structure of reality is binary and our knowledge of the world is essentially bi-focal. This theory, which makes good and evil totally interdependent, Augustine set aside for a more abstract, subtle theory.

Years after the *Confessions* Augustine summarised his beliefs in his small compendium of Christian teaching, the *Enchiridion*:

> What, after all, is anything we call evil but the privation of good? In animal bodies, for instance, sickness and wounds are nothing but

the privation of health. When a cure is effected, the evils which were present (i.e. the sickness and the wounds) do not retreat and go elsewhere, they simply do not exist any more. For such evil is not a substance; the wound or the disease is a defect of the bodily substance which, as a Substance, is good. Evil, then, is called an accident, i.e. a privation of that good which is called health.

In this way Augustine solved two troubling problems. First, if evil did not 'exist', God could not be held responsible for it. Secondly, by calling it the absence of good, the sovereignty of the Almighty in the universe was preserved: there could be no other Principle or Being that was creating structures and situations beyond his power. But while it solved some problems it created others.

It may have entered the intellect of Western theology as the most plausible explanation of evil, but it failed to capture the Christian imagination: it seemed preposterously abstract to those who did not live their lives at the level of philosophical abstraction. And, it has to be admitted, Augustine's Neoplatonic vocabulary fitted awkwardly with much of the traditional Christian teaching about evil. 'Do you renounce the devil and all his works?' asks the interrogator at the rite of Baptism. And those about to be baptised answer: 'We do.' But who, then, is this devil, and where are his works? If evil is only an absence, it cannot be imagined and certainly cannot be personified.

If Christianity were nothing more than a philosophical system, a collection of abstract speculations, the theory of evil as *privatio boni* would be perfectly acceptable. It would not have to be imagined – and we have seen how dangerously close Augustine came to wanting to free Christianity from 'bodily imaginings'. Here the Neoplatonic influence is at its most insidious. But this is not the way in which a religion (except, possibly, Buddhism) works. Religion captures the whole of life, it articulates the new life in prayer and worship, movement and ritual, story and prophecy. The imagination will play at least as large a part as the intellect. Even Islam, that way of life most wary of idolatry and most severe in its condemnation of the making of images, has a holy book replete with sensuous imagery, including, of course, images of evil vividly presented.

So it is with Christianity. Despite the fact that, at the level of theological discourse, Augustine's account of the nature of evil was received into the tradition and became widely accepted as orthodox belief, depictions of evil in thousands of guises appeared everywhere; in illuminated manuscripts and carvings; on the walls of churches; in the movements of the liturgy; in sermons and meditations and poetry. The dualism which Augustine had so deliberately and ingeniously avoided burst out in a multitude of images in the centuries that followed. It would need more than the brilliance of Augustine's theology to eradicate the experience of evil as a reality. Evil was felt as fact, something known and feared. How, it was implicitly asked in the hundreds of thousands of pictures that surrounded ordinary lives and expressed ordinary reactions, could one have an experience of something that did not exist? The closing petition of the Lord's Prayer sounded unnecessary, or at least melodramatic, when evil was interpreted in this way. Was one praying to be delivered from nothing? No, whatever Augustine may have said, as far as the vast majority of ordinary Christians were concerned, evil existed and could be portrayed in words and pictures: the fight against it was real, the prayers about deliverance from it were genuine and fervent.

But perhaps this account of Augustine's theory of evil is inadequate. How could a man who so clearly felt the misery as well as the splendour of life leave his explanation of the problem of evil at the level of Neoplatonist philosophy? The answer is: he could not and did not. 'In Augustine's Christianity, the sense of sin is the narrow gate through which all must pass who would see the truth . . . No one can say "Evil be thou my good"; the lie that every man utters in the moment of sin is that evil is his good' (John Burnaby). He returned to the problem over and over again in sermons, treatises, letters and commentaries trying to construct a theory that was not only comprehensive and intelligible, but true to experience and faith. He ran into almost insurmountable difficulties. How was one to deal with the notion of cosmic evil? Like almost everyone of his age, he accepted without question the existence of the devil and the legions of fallen angels. He held firmly to the belief that Christ's death and resurrection was the victory over sin and the deliverance from the power of supernatural evil. But he remained disconcertingly vague on the difficult question of why angelic beings should have turned away from goodness and light and plunged into darkness and rebellion, and why they should have the power to imprison the hearts and minds of men and women. He often spoke of demonic creatures as though they were objective forces of evil, but failed, satisfactorily, to explain how a 'no-thing' could be a force. Above all, there was the question of Satan. According to his theory, evil was ultimately self-defeating and could accomplish nothing; a totally evil being could not exist, by definition. The arguments went round and round and in and out. Was Satan, perhaps, to be regarded as having retained in himself some elements of goodness, even in his fallenness? Could he, therefore, be redeemed – as one of Augustine's great predecessors,

Origen, had argued? This he denied. On and on he went, searching for answers.

...

For more than a decade after the sack of the imperial city of Rome by the Visigoths in 410 Augustine laboured on his extraordinary work, *The City of God*. In Book XI he addresses the problem of evil again, but not before he has considered the nature of creation:

> For leaving aside the utterances of the prophets, we have the evidence of the world itself in all its ordered change and movement and in all the beauty it presents to our sight, a world which bears a kind of silent testimony to the fact of its creation, and proclaims that its maker could have been none other than God, the ineffably and invisibly great, the ineffably and invisibly beautiful.

The clue we are looking for is to be found in the words 'ordered change and movement'. If evil is defined as *privatio* or absence, we may ask: an absence of what? The answer comes back, 'good', *privatio boni*. Is this sufficient explanation? In what does this goodness consist, and how should we recognise it? Augustine answers in terms of order: of things being in a right relation to one another. Without order there would be chaos and we could know nothing; without order there could be no unity, for it is only in a proper ordering that disparate things may be united without confusion or destruction. Order is the characteristic of the work and love of God, of creation and redemption. Disorder is the sign of sin: evil is the privation, the absence of, order. Over and over again he prays that the disordered wills of human beings may be so governed by the Spirit of God that they will be reordered and given that which they lack, and were deprived of, before. His view of the original creation was of a glorious ordering of the constituent parts of the universe; his view of fallen creation was, conversely, a view of the disruption of that order. Each human being is evil – that is, disordered: the appetites at war with the intellect; the bodily parts at war with themselves, resulting in disfigurement and disease. Human society – the city – is disordered; men and women in conflict out of greed, envy or lust. The order of the heavenly hierarchy had been disrupted by the rebellion of Satan.

> And so the Devil did not stand firm in the truth, and yet he did not escape the judgement of the truth. He did not continue in the

tranquility of order; but that did not mean he escaped from the power of the imposer of order.

There is an order to be known, loved and accepted. Disordered love is love of the lesser instead of the greater; the preference of the lower to the higher; resting content with earthly delights; being satisfied with the beauty of this world instead of the beauty of God. (This puts into perspective Augustine's ambivalent attitude to 'bodily images'.) The absence of order – the attempted perversion of what *is* – can be felt and depicted even while, paradoxically, we can say that it is an absence. To attempt to embrace the impossible and make it real is to say 'Evil be thou my good' and to try to make it so. But because evil has no real being, one wills oneself out of existence: hell is populated with those who have tried to live by illusion, by a lie, by pretending that nothing is something.

3.5 The free will defence

[*According to the Freewill Defence (FWD), moral evil is the risk God must take in creating freedom of the will. On this view, God could not have created free people who were guaranteed always to do the right thing. Most of those who appeal to the FWD adopt 'libertarianism', which is the view that some human acts are not wholly determined by causal laws and thus predictable, but are the responsibility of free agents. 'Soft determinists' (eg. Flew and Mackie), however, argue that to be 'free' is only to be free of 'external constraint', and therefore that we are free even though our choosing and acting are completely predictable because they are completely determined (i.e. we could not have decided/acted differently). For them, free will is compatible with determinism. Hence they argue, against the FWD, that God could have given everyone a good character which was always expressed in good actions (see Hick's response, below). ('Hard determinists', by contrast, believe not only in the truth of determinism but also that it is incompatible with notions of freedom and responsibility, and therefore that moral judgements of 'good' and 'evil are inappropriate.)*]

John Hick, *Philosophy of Religion*, **Englewood Cliffs, New Jersey, Prentice-Hall, 1983, p. 42**

If by free actions we mean actions that are not externally compelled but flow from the nature of agents as they react to the circumstances in which they find themselves, then there is indeed no contradiction between our being free and our actions' being 'caused' (by our own God-given nature) and thus being in principle predictable. However, it is suggested, there is a contradiction in saying that *God* is the cause of our acting as we do *and* that we are free beings specifically in relation to God. The contradiction is between holding that God has so made us that we shall of necessity act in a certain way, and that we are genuinely independent persons *in relation to God*. If all our thoughts and actions are divinely predestined, then however free and responsible we may seem to ourselves to be, we are not free and responsible in the sight of God but must instead be God's puppets. Such 'freedom' would be comparable to that of patients acting out a series of posthypnotic suggestions: they appear to themselves to be free, but their volitions have actually been predetermined by the will of the hypnotist, in relation to whom the patients are therefore not genuinely free agents. Thus, it is suggested, while God *could* have created such beings, there would have been no point in doing so – at least not if God is seeking to create sons and daughters rather than human puppets.

Alvin Plantinga, *God, Freedom and Evil*, London, George Allen & Unwin, 1975, pp. 30–2, 53

We can make a preliminary statement of the Free Will Defense as follows. A world containing creatures who are significantly free (and freely perform more good than evil actions) is more valuable, all else being equal, than a world containing no free creatures at all. Now God can create free creatures, but He can't *cause* or *determine* them to do only what is right. For if He does so, then they aren't significantly free after all; they do not do what is right *freely*. To create creatures capable of *moral good*, therefore, He must create creatures capable of moral evil; and He can't give these creatures the freedom to perform evil and at the same time prevent them from doing so. As it turned out, sadly enough, some of the free creatures God created went wrong in the exercise of their freedom; this is the source of moral evil. The fact that free creatures sometimes go wrong, however, counts neither against God's omnipotence nor against His goodness; for He could have forestalled the occurrence of moral evil only by removing the possibility of moral good.

I said earlier that the Free Will Defender tries to find a proposition that is consistent with

(1)   God is omniscient, omnipotent, and wholly good

and together with (1) entails that there is evil. According to the Free Will Defense, we must find this proposition somewhere in the above story.

The varieties of theodicy

The heart of the Free Will Defense is the claim that it is *possible* that God could not have created a universe containing moral good (or as much moral good as this world contains) without creating one that also contained moral evil. And if so, then it is possible that God has a good reason for creating a world containing evil.

Now this defense has met with several kinds of objections. For example, some philosophers say that *causal determinism* and *freedom*, contrary to what we might have thought, are not really incompatible. But if so, then God could have created free creatures who were free, and free to do what is wrong, but nevertheless were causally determined to do only what is right. Thus He could have created creatures who were free to do what was wrong, while nevertheless preventing them from ever performing any wrong actions – simply by seeing to it that they were causally determined to do only what is right. Of course this contradicts the Free Will Defense, according to which there is inconsistency in supposing that God determines free creatures to do only what is right. But is it really possible that all of a person's actions are causally determined while some of them are free? How could that be so? According to one version of the doctrine in question, to say that George acts freely on a given occasion is to say only this: *if George had chosen to do otherwise, he would have done otherwise*. Now George's action *A* is causally determined if some event *E* – some event beyond his control – has already occurred, where the state of affairs consisting in *E*'s occurrence conjoined with George's *refraining* from performing *A*, is a causally impossible state of affairs. Then one can consistently hold both that all of a man's actions are causally determined and that some of them are free in the above sense. For suppose that all of a man's actions are causally determined and that he *couldn't*, on any occasion, have made any choice or performed any action different from the ones he did make and perform. It could still be true that if he *had* chosen to do otherwise, he would have done otherwise. Granted, he couldn't have chosen to do otherwise; but this is consistent with saying that *if* he had, things would have gone differently.

This objection to the Free Will Defense seems utterly implausible. One might as well claim that being in jail doesn't really limit one's freedom on the grounds that if one were *not* in jail, he'd be free to come and go as he pleased. So I shall say no more about this objection here.

A second objection is more formidable. In essence it goes like this. Surely it is possible to do only what is right, even if one is free to do wrong. It is *possible*, in that broadly logical sense, that there be a world containing free creatures who always do what is right. There is certainly no *contradiction* or *inconsistency* in this idea. But God is omnipotent; his power has no nonlogical limitations. So if it's possible that there be a world containing creatures who are free to do what is wrong but never in fact do so, then it follows that an omnipotent God could create such a world.

. . .

[T]he interesting fact here is this: it is possible that every creaturely essence – every essence including the property of being created by God – suffers from transworld depravity [*i.e. in any possible world in which she/he exists, she/he will do some evil*]. But now suppose this is true. Now God can create a world containing moral good only by creating significantly free persons. And, since every person is the instantiation of an essence, He can create significantly free persons only by instantiating some essences. But if every essence suffers from transworld depravity, then no matter which essences God instantiates, the resulting persons, if free with respect to morally significant actions, would always perform at least some wrong actions. If every essence suffers from transworld depravity, then it was beyond the power of God Himself to create a world containing moral good but no moral evil. He might have been able to create worlds in which moral evil is very considerably outweighed by moral good; but it was not within His power to create worlds containing moral good but no moral evil – and this despite the fact that He is omnipotent. Under these conditions God could have created a world containing no moral evil only by creating one without significantly free persons. But it is possible that every essence suffers from transworld depravity; so it's possible that God could not have created a world containing moral good but no moral evil.

Keith Ward, *Religion and Human Nature*, Oxford, Oxford University Press, 1998, pp. 159–60, 162, 179–80, 183–4

[*The free will defence has not only been appealed to as an explanation of individual acts of human wrong-doing. In the Augustinian tradition of theodicy it is also used to explain the tendency to sin – 'original sin' – that we are said to inherit as a consequence of Adam's Fall. Some have claimed that we also inherit personal guilt for that Fall, and even that natural evil may be thought of as a just punishment for it.*]

The biblical narrative of Adam and Eve in the Garden of Eden may seem to be completely outdated by the evolutionary account of human genesis.

After all, if one takes the Genesis narrative literally, humans were directly created by God in about 4004 BCE, and lived in a state of bliss and knowledge of God in a world without death or suffering. When they disobeyed God they were punished by having to cultivate the earth in hardship and bear children in suffering, and so death entered the world. This contrasts sharply with the evolutionist account of humans evolving from other species, and achieving their dominant position on earth by the exercise of a lust and aggression which become necessary conditions of their survival in a competitive environment. Death and suffering existed for millennia before humans arrived on the scene, and the first humans were probably ignorant, barbaric, and religiously primitive. The idea of a 'fall' from grace seems to have been replaced by the idea of a hesitant, ambiguous, and only partly successful 'rise' towards moral and rational action.

The contrast is not in fact as great as this suggests. The Genesis narrative is usually interpreted in recent theology as primarily symbolic of the human situation, rather than as literally descriptive. It is most plausibly taken in the same way that one takes myths of origin from other primal traditions, as an imaginative and putatively inspired symbolization of the fundamental elements of the human situation. If one does that, Adam, which can simply mean 'person' in Hebrew, becomes the symbol of humanity, and Eden, 'bliss', is the ideal intended state of human existence. Humanity is intended to know and love God, and to care for the earth in harmony and joy. When Adam takes the fruit of the tree of knowledge against God's command, what is being pointed to is a basic flaw in human knowledge and understanding. Humans seek knowledge before they are ready for it, they seek knowledge without responsibility, and use it for self-regarding purposes. Their misuse of knowledge leads to profound spiritual death, separation from knowledge of and friendship with God. It leads to the institution of work as drudgery, to the creation of forms of social oppression and to a sense of estrangement from the environment and from other sentient life.

This is a profound analysis of the human condition, and it is quite compatible with the evolutionist account of human biological origins. As is common in primal origin stories, the concern is not with what happened at the beginning of human history, but with the condition of every human being in relation to the environment and to God. The 'beginning' is the intended ideal and the 'Fall' is the flawed human condition, which makes that ideal apparently impossible of achievement, though it remains the true human goal.

. . .

The most appealing account of these matters in early Christian thought is perhaps that of Irenaeus, who spoke of the first humans as infants, made in the image of God, who were meant to grow by their own co-operation with divine grace into the likeness of God. The Fall consisted in the loss of the sense of a felt unity with the sacred root of being, in the inability to co-operate with its gracious guidance, and so in the growth of that sense of solitude and estrangement which becomes the lot of humanity in a state of sin. The 'banishment from Eden' is the sense of human solitude and weakness that is the consequence of the human attempt to grasp at power without responsible love. The human desire for self-determination becomes a human determination towards self-regard. Therein lies the paradoxical tragedy of human existence, that it is precisely self-regard which leads to the destruction of the self. Human society is a society set on a course of self-destruction, and unless self-regard can be eradicated at its root, there can be no health either for individuals or for society. That is the heart of the doctrine of 'original sin'.

. . .

In the Christian tradition, the idea of original sin has often been merged with that of original guilt and given a moralistic interpretation, as it was in Augustine. Each human child, at the moment it is born, is then seen as inheriting a sense of guilt, as being deserving of damnation, before it has even performed any action. Its will is corrupt and blameworthy, and it is perfectly just of God to punish it eternally, or to forgive it, if that happens to be the divine pleasure. Augustine writes: 'In committing so great a sin their [the first parents'] whole nature, being hereby depraved . . . was so transfused through all their offspring in the same degree of corruption and necessity of death . . . that all would have been cast headlong into the second death . . . had not the undue grace of God acquitted some from it' (*City of God*, 14. I). All human children are born with a depraved nature, and justly suffer for the sin of their first ancestor.

. . .

One needs to reject, on moral grounds, the idea that children are born guilty. One needs to reject, on scientific grounds, the ideas that moral fault can be inherited, and that some fundamental genetic change in humans could be caused by a primeval sin.

Nevertheless, the Augustinian tradition was expressing, however misleadingly, an insight into the human condition. Humans do seem to be burdened with weakened and corrupted wills, and this makes it impossible for them to enter into that community of shared experience and action that is God's intention for creation. Moreover, the moralism that concentrates only on the individual's achievement of moral success misses an important dimension of human existence.

. . .

It is . . . plausible to hold that, because of the early moral failures of many humans, the whole human world has become entrapped in egoism and estranged from a sense of the presence of God. The loss of the vision of God is indeed the natural consequence for individuals born into such a world. In that sense, one may construe the belief that 'humans are born guilty' as the assertion that the natural destiny of ungraced human nature is the punishment of loveless existence, which is Hell. It may be true that the natural human situation falls under divine judgement. But that can only be said when it is equally clearly seen that it also, and from the very first, falls under the divine mercy: 'God has consigned all men to disobedience, that he may have mercy upon all' (Romans 11:32). If this is so, it cannot be held that by baptism, and only by baptism, 'the guilt of original sin is remitted', as the Council of Trent held. Yet one can say that only by God's grace can relationship to God be restored. This grace is universally available to all, and must be appropriated by personal response. Baptism is the sign that such grace comes as an offer to all, that it is normatively mediated in a community patterned on Christ, and that the church as a community truly mediates the life of Christ, who has opened a new and living way to relationship with God.

3.6 The vale of soul-making

[*On this view, natural evil is a necessary component of creation if the world is to provide an environment in which free human beings can develop morally. This may be argued for three reasons.*

(i) *To be 'good', human beings must be liable to temptation, not immunized from evil.*
(ii) *The world is not intended as a 'hedonistic paradise', but as an environment for moral growth. Courage, compassion and other virtues would not develop in a world where there was no suffering and no danger.*
(iii) *If God were always intervening in the world to prevent the consequences of our moral evil, not only would the world become too unpredictable for independent action, but our 'wrong' acts would also*

never have 'bad' consequences – and we should therefore never develop a sense of the wrongness of our evil intentions.]

John Hick, *Evil and the God of Love*, London, Collins, 1968, pp. 291–4, 297, 370–1

The value-judgement that is implicitly being invoked here is that one who has attained to goodness by meeting and eventually mastering temptations, and thus by rightly making responsible choices in concrete situations, is good in a richer and more valuable sense than would be one created *ab initio* in a state either of innocence or of virtue.

. . .

Antitheistic writers almost invariably assume a conception of the divine purpose which is contrary to the Christian conception. They assume that the purpose of a loving God must be to create a hedonistic paradise; and therefore to the extent that the world is other than this, it proves to them that God is either not loving enough or not powerful enough to create such a world. They think of God's relation to the earth on the model of a human being building a cage for a pet animal to dwell in. If he is humane he will naturally make his pet's quarters as pleasant and healthful as he can. Any respect in which the cage falls short of the veterinarian's ideal, and contains possibilities of accident or disease, is evidence of either limited benevolence or limited means, or both. Those who use the problem of evil as an argument against belief in God almost invariably think of the world in this kind of way. David Hume, for example, speaks of an architect who is trying to plan a house that is to be as comfortable and convenient as possible. If we find that 'the windows, doors, fires, passages, stairs, and the whole economy of the building were the source of noise, confusion, fatigue, darkness, and the extremes of heat and cold' we should have no hesitation in blaming the architect. It would be in vain for him to prove that if this or that defect were corrected greater ills would result: 'still you would assert in general, that, if the architect had had skill and good intentions, he might have formed such a plan of the whole and might have adjusted the parts in such a manner, as would have remedied all or most of these inconveniences' (*Dialogues Concerning Natural Religion*, part XI).

. . .

Such critics as Hume are confusing what heaven ought to be, as an environment for perfected finite beings, with what this world ought to be, as an environment for beings who are in process of becoming perfected. For if our general conception of God's purpose is correct the world is not intended to be a paradise, but rather the scene of a history in which human personality may be formed towards the pattern of Christ. Men are not to be thought of on the analogy of animal pets, whose life is to be made as agreeable as possible, but rather on the analogy of human children, who are to grow to adulthood in an environment whose primary and overriding purpose is not immediate pleasure but the realizing of the most valuable potentialities of human personality.

...

This, then, is the starting-point from which we propose to try to relate the realities of sin and suffering to the perfect love of an omnipotent Creator. And as will become increasingly apparent, a theodicy that starts in this way must be eschatological in its ultimate bearings. That is to say, instead of looking to the past for its clue to the mystery of evil, it looks to the future, and indeed to that ultimate future to which only faith can look. Given the conception of a divine intention working in and through human time towards a fulfilment that lies in its completeness beyond human time, our theodicy must find the meaning of evil in the part that it is made to play in the eventual outworking of that purpose; and must find the justification of the whole process in the magnitude of the good to which it leads. The good that outshines all ill is not a paradise long since lost but a kingdom which is yet to come in its full glory and permanence.

...

Try to imagine a world which, although not entirely free from pain and suffering, nevertheless contained no unjust and undeserved or excessive and apparently dysteleological misery [*that is, misery that lacks a point or purpose*]. Although there would be sufficient hardships and dangers and problems to give spice to life, there would be no utterly destructive and apparently vindictive evil. On the contrary, men's sufferings would always be seen either to be justly deserved punishments or else to serve a constructive purpose of moral training.

In such a world human misery would not evoke deep personal sympathy or call forth organized relief and sacrificial help and service. For it is presupposed in these compassionate reactions both that the suffering is not deserved and that it is *bad* for the sufferer.... It seems, then, that in a world that is to be the scene of compassionate love and self-giving for others, suffering must fall upon mankind with something of the haphazardness and inequity that we now experience. It must be apparently unmerited, pointless, and incapable of being morally rationalized. For it is precisely this feature of our common human lot that creates sympathy between man and man and evokes the unselfish kindness and goodwill which are among the highest values of personal life. No undeserved need would mean no uncalculating outpouring to meet that need.

Topics for discussion

1. What do philosophers mean by 'the problem of evil'? What would they regard as constituting a 'solution'? Do such 'solutions' impose constraints upon God, or is logic not appropriately seen as a constraint?
2. What may be seen as the principal advantages and disadvantages of the Augustinian and Irenaean types of approach to theodicy?
3. May the principle of plenitude be used to explain the variety in the world? Is it the sort of variety one would expect of a creator?
4. What is freedom? Is it worth the candle?
5. What is meant by 'transworld depravity'? Why does Plantinga think it necessary to consider possible worlds?
6. Is it helpful to think of this world as a vale of soul-making?
7. Can the doctrine of 'original sin' help to solve the problem of evil?

4 The logic of theodicy

4.1 The best possible world?

M. B. Ahern, *The Problem of Evil*, London, Routledge & Kegan Paul, 1971, pp. 59–61

Leibniz believed that the existence of God can be established independently of evil. Consequently, problems about God and evil are in no way problems about God's existence but problems of how to account for evil since an omnipotent and wholly good God exists. He tried to solve these problems by claiming that all actual evil is a necessary element in the best possible world. Because it is a necessary means to the greatest good, the world's evil is justified.

Leibniz believed that this world is the best world possible, not on empirical but on theoretical grounds. God would make only the best possible world. He was free to create an unlimited variety of world or to create none, but if He created He would make only the best world. No agent acts rationally unless he has sufficient reason for what he does. Because God is both infinitely wise and good, the only sufficient reason He could have for choosing a world is that the sum of its perfection is the greatest possible.

Were other less good worlds really possible and was God really free to choose this one, since He must act for a sufficient reason? Could there be a sufficient reason for choosing any other world than the best possible? Leibniz's answer is that the creation of this world was not logically or metaphysically necessary but that it was morally necessary and certain to take place . . .

. . .

In any event, Leibniz's main claim that in making this world, God must have made the best possible world, remains intact. An obvious argument against it is the existence of evil. Leibniz does not attempt to deny its existence. He says that evil contributes to the world's perfection in such a way that, without it, the world would not be the best possible. The reason is that 'the best alternative is not always that which tends to avoid evil, since it can happen that evil may be accompanied by a greater good'; and 'Not only does (God) derive from (evils) greater goods, but He finds them connected with the greatest goods of all those that are possible; so that it would be a fault not to permit them.'

For Leibniz, then, the best possible world is not a perfect world, that is, a world free of all imperfection. It must contain the evil which the present world had in the past, does have now, and will have in the future for without it a world which, taken as a whole, is the best possible, would not exist. Consequently, the answer to all of the concrete problems of evil, as Leibniz understands them, is that in every case, actual evil is a necessary means to greater good and, ultimately, to the greatest good.

[*Confidence that this was the 'best of all possible worlds', which was given its most famous philosophical defence in Leibniz'* Theodicy *of 1710, received a severe shock with the Lisbon earthquake of 1755. Tens of thousands were killed, many of whom were in church, it being All Saints Day. None the less, for Christian and non-Christian alike, the issue often continues today to be debated in the same way, as the extracts below from Mackie (atheist) and Davis (Christian) illustrate.*]

John L. Mackie, *The Miracle of Theism: Arguments For and Against the Existence of God*, Oxford, Oxford University Press, 1982, pp. 153–5

Much more interesting than this is the suggestion that things that are evil in themselves may contribute to the goodness of an 'organic whole' in which they are found, so that the world as a whole is better as it is, with some evils in it, than it could be if there were no evil.

. . .

This solution usually starts from the assumption that the evil whose existence constitutes the problem of evil is primarily what is called physical evil, that is, pain, suffering, and disease. If this is taken as the difficulty, the theist can reply that these things make possible the existence of sympathy, kindness, heroism, and the gradually successful struggle of doctors, reformers, and so on to overcome these evils. Indeed, theists often seize the opportunity to accuse those who raise the problem of taking a low, materialist view of good and evil, equating these with pleasure and pain, and of ignoring the more spiritual goods which arise, and can only arise, in the struggle against evils.

. . .

This is a particularly subtle attempt to solve the problem. It defends God's goodness and omnipotence on the ground that (on a long enough view) this is the best of all possible worlds, because it includes the important second-order goods [*i.e. those goods such as sympathy and courage which would not exist unless pain and suffering existed*], and yet it admits that real evils, namely the first-order ones, occur. It reconciles these apparently incompatible theses by, in effect, modifying one of our additional premises. It denies that a wholly good being would eliminate evil as far as he could, but explains this denial by pointing to a reason why a being who is wholly good, in a sense that is thoroughly intelligible to us and coherent with the ordinary concept of goodness, might not eliminate evils, even though it was logically possible to do so and though he was able to do whatever is logically possible, and was limited only by the logical impossibility of having the second-order good without the first-order evil.

Since this defence is formally possible, and its principle involves no real abandonment of our ordinary view of the opposition between good and evil, we can concede that the problem of evil does not, after all, show that the central doctrines of theism are logically inconsistent with one another. But whether this offers a real solution of the problem is another question. Let us call an evil which is explained and justified in the proposed way an *absorbed* evil. For example, some bit of suffering which is actually the object of kindness or sympathy whose goodness outweighs the badness of that suffering itself will be an absorbed evil, as will be miseries or injustices that are in fact progressively overcome by a struggle whose nobility is a higher good which outweighs the evils without which it could not have occurred. What this defence shows, then, is that the existence of completely absorbed evils is compatible with the existence of an omnipotent and wholly good god. But then the vital question is this: can the theist maintain that the only evils that occur in the world are absorbed evils? When this question is squarely put, it is surely plain that he cannot. On the one hand there are surplus first-order evils, suffering and the like which are not actually used in any good organic whole, and on the other there are second-order evils; these will not be incorporated in second-order goods, but will contrast with them: malevolence, cruelty, callousness, cowardice, and states of affairs in which there is not progress but decline, where things get worse rather than better. The problem, therefore, now recurs as the problem of unabsorbed evils, and we have as yet no way of reconciling their existence with that of a god of the traditional sort.

Robert Merrihew Adams, 'Must God Create the Best?', *Philosophical Review*, LXXXI, 3, 1972, pp. 317–19, 323–4

Many philosophers and theologians have accepted the following proposition:

(P) If a perfectly good moral agent created any world at all, it would have to be the very best world that he could create.

The best world that an omnipotent God could create is the best of all logically possible worlds. Accordingly, it has been supposed that if the actual world was created by an omnipotent, perfectly good God, it must be the best of all logically possible worlds.

In this paper I shall argue that ethical views typical of the Judeo-Christian religious tradition do not require the Judeo-Christian theist to accept (P). He must hold that the actual world is a good world. But he need not maintain that it is the best of all possible worlds, or the best world that God could have made.

The position which I am claiming that he can consistently hold is that *even if* there is a best among possible worlds, God could create another instead of it, and still be perfectly good.

. . .

Whether we accept proposition (P) will depend on what we believe are the requirements for perfect goodness. If we apply an act-utilitarian standard of moral goodness, we will have to accept (P). For by act-utilitarian standards it is a moral obligation to bring about the best state of affairs that one can. It is interesting to note that the ethics of Leibniz, the best-known advocate of (P), is basically utilitarian. In his *Theodicy* (Part I, Section 25) he maintains, in effect, that men, because of their ignorance of many of the consequences of their actions, ought to follow a rule-utilitarian code, but that God, being omniscient, must be a perfect act utilitarian in order to be perfectly good. [*Adams means by 'act utilitarianism' behaving so as to maximize on each occasion the sum total of pleasure and pain, and by 'rule utilitarianism' following general moral rules which themselves have a utilitarian justification.*]

I believe that utilitarian views are not typical of the Judeo-Christian ethical tradition, although Leibniz is by no means the only Christian utilitarian. In this essay I shall assume that we are working with standards of moral goodness which are not utilitarian.

. . .

Is there someone *to* whom a creator would have an obligation to create the best world he could?

. . .

Might he have an obligation to the creatures in the best possible world, to create them? Have they been wronged, or even treated unkindly, if God has created a less excellent world, in which they do not exist, instead of creating them? I think not. The difference between actual beings and merely possible beings is of fundamental moral importance here. The moral community consists of actual beings. It is they who have actual rights, and it is to them that there are actual obligations. A merely possible being cannot be (actually) wronged or treated unkindly. A being who never exists is not wronged by not being created, and there is no obligation to any possible being to bring it into existence.

. . .

Plato is one of those who held that a perfectly good creator would make the very best world he could. He thought that if the creator chose to make a world less good than he could have made, that could be understood only in terms of some defect in the creator's character. Envy is the defect that Plato suggests. It may be thought that the creation of a world inferior to the best that he could make would manifest a defect in the creator's character even if no one were thereby wronged or treated unkindly. For the perfectly good moral agent must not only be kind and refrain from violating the rights of others, but must also have other virtues. For instance, he must be noble, generous, high-minded, and free from envy. He must satisfy the moral ideal.

There are differences of opinion, however, about what is to be included in the moral ideal. One important element in the Judeo-Christian moral ideal is *grace*. For present purposes, grace may be defined as a disposition to love which is not dependent on the merit of the person loved. The gracious person loves without worrying about whether the person he loves is worthy of his love. Or perhaps it would be better to say that the gracious person sees what is valuable in the person he loves, and does not worry about whether it is more or less valuable than what could be found in someone else he might have loved. In the

Judeo-Christian tradition it is typically believed that grace is a virtue which God does have and men ought to have.

A God who is gracious with respect to creating might well choose to create and love less excellent creatures than He could have chosen. This is not to suggest that grace in creation consists in a preference for imperfection as such. God could have chosen to create the best of all possible creatures, and still have been gracious in choosing them. God's graciousness in creation does not imply that the creatures He has chosen to create must be less excellent than the best possible. It implies, rather, that even if they are the best possible creatures, that is not the ground for His choosing them. And it implies that there is nothing in God's nature or character which would require Him to act on the principle of choosing the best possible creatures to be the object of His creative powers.

Grace, as I have described it, is not part of everyone's moral ideal. For instance, it was not part of Plato's moral ideal. The thought that it may be the expression of a virtue, rather than a defect of character, in a creator, *not* to act on the principle of creating the best creatures he possibly could, is quite foreign to Plato's ethical viewpoint. But I believe that thought is not at all foreign to a Judeo-Christian ethical viewpoint.

4.2 Maximizing satisfaction?

George N. Schlesinger, 'Suffering and Evil', in Steven M. Cahn and David Shatz (eds), *Contemporary Philosophy of Religion*, New York, Oxford University Press, 1982, pp. 27–30

On the surface, it may seem that my obligation toward another is to make him as happy as I can, provided this does not interfere with the welfare of others. Upon reflection, however, this appears inadequate.

Suppose I have under my care a child of very low intelligence but of very happy disposition. Provided his basic bodily needs are minimally taken care of, he enjoys lying on his back all day long and staring into the air. A minor operation, I am assured by the best medical authorities, would spectacularly raise his intelligence and render him capable of creative achievements as well as the appreciation of music, art, literature, and science. Naturally, if his intelligence were raised he would be vulnerable to the frustrations, disappointments, and anxieties most of us are subject to from time to time. Nevertheless, I believe it will be agreed that I should be reprehensible if I refrained from letting the child have the operation, even if I insured to the best of my ability that his physical needs would always be taken care of.

But why is it not good enough that I am keeping him in a state of maximum happiness? Apparently, the degree of desirability of a state is not a simple function of a single factor – namely, the degree to which one's wants are satisfied – but is also dependent on the kind of being one is. The somewhat less happy but intelligent child is ultimately better off than the happy idiot because, although the amount of happiness is less in his case, he is more than compensated for this by having become a preferable kind of person.

Thus, my moral obligations do not consist simply in having to endeavor to raise the amount of happiness a certain being is granted to enjoy. These obligations are somewhat more complex and consist in my having to raise the degree of desirability of his state, a two-valued function depending both on the potentials of the individual and the extent to which his needs are being taken care of. The idea may be illustrated as follows. In recent years much has been heard about machines that electrically stimulate the pleasure centers of one's brain. Once a person's brain is connected to the machine, he becomes completely captivated by the experience it provides and desires absolutely nothing but the passive enjoyment of the sublime pleasures it induces. But I believe that most would condemn me if, without prior consultation, I hooked up A, a normal person, to this machine and thus caused him to become addicted to it for the rest of his life.

. . .

Even if the needs of others are not taken into account, it will be agreed by most that by inducing in A a permanent state of euphoria I have not done a good thing to him. This is so because I have reduced the desirability of A's state. The latter is not solely a function of how satiated A is with pleasure but also of the kind of being he is. A was, prior to my interference, capable of a great variety of response, of interaction with others, of creativity and self-improvement, while now he is reduced to a completely inactive, vegetable-like existence. The great increase in the factor of happiness is insufficient to make up for the great loss in the second factor, A's being lowered from the state of a normal human being to the state of an inferior quasi-hibernating inert existence.

. . .

Now I take it that conceptually there is no limit to the degree which the desirability of a person's state may reach. One can easily conceive a super-Socrates who has a much higher intelligence and many more than five senses through which to enjoy the world and who stands to Socrates as the latter stands to the pig. And there is the possibility of a super-super-Socrates and so on *ad infinitum*. Given this last supposition about an infinite hierarchy of possible beings and hence the limitlessness of the possible increase in the degree of desirability of state, how does the universal ethical rule, '... increase the degree of desirability of state as much as possible,' apply to God? After all, no matter to what degree it is increased it is always logically possible to increase it further. A mortal's possibilities are physically limited, hence in his case there is a natural limit to the principle; but there is no limit to what God can do. It is therefore logically impossible for Him to fulfill the ethical principle, i.e., to do enough to discharge His obligation to do more and further increase the degree of desirability of state. But what is logically impossible to do cannot be done by an omnipotent being either, and it is agreed by practically all philosophers that God's inability to do what is logically impossible does not diminish His omnipotence. Just as it is logically impossible to name the highest integer, it is impossible to grant a creature a degree of desirability of state higher than which is inconceivable; thus it is logically impossible for God to fulfill what is required by the universal ethical principle, and therefore He cannot fulfill it, and so is not obliged to fulfill it. There is no room for complaint, seeing that God has not fulfilled the ethical principle which mortals are bound by and has left His creatures in various low states of desirability. Thus the problem of evil vanishes.

...

[An] objection a sceptic might want to raise is that while nobody can reach the logical limit of happiness, there seem to be no conceptual obstacles against at least eliminating all possible misery. He could therefore challenge the theist and say that if God were good, then at least He should not have permitted any creature, however exalted or humble its kind, to be positively distressed at any time.

But once we have agreed on the reasonableness of the value judgment expounded in the previous section, it necessarily follows that it is possible for *A* to be really much better off than *B* even though *A* is dissatisfied and *B* satisfied. For *A*, who may be deficient in one of the ingredients that contribute to the desirability of his condition – namely in happiness, may have been more than sufficiently compensated by having been granted the other ingredient in abundance, i.e., by having been allotted a much higher rank in the hierarchy of beings. Thus we can see the absurdity of the sceptic's position. Confronted with *B*, he sees no grounds to question Divine goodness, since *B* does not suffer. But should God *improve*

B's lot and raise the degree of the desirability of his state to be equal to that of *A*, this he would regard as evil!

4.3 Necessary evil?
Richard Swinburne, *The Existence of God*, Oxford, Oxford University Press, 1979, pp. 202–8

I turn now to an argument that the existence of many natural evils of the kind described is logically necessary for the existence of a world of the type which I have already described. For they are necessary if agents are to have the *knowledge* of how to bring about evil or prevent its occurrence, knowledge which they must have if they are to have a genuine choice between bringing about evil and bringing about good.

. . .

Now if agents are knowingly to bring about states of affairs, or to allow states of affairs to come about through neglecting to prevent them, they must know what consequences will follow from their actions. Normal inductive knowledge of consequences . . . is to be obtained as follows. Consider an action *A* which I am contemplating doing in circumstances *X*. Suppose that *A* consists in bringing about a state of affairs *C*, the result of *A*. How am I to know what its effects will be, what will follow from it? Most certainly, by having done such an action myself many times before in similar circumstances, and having observed the effects of its result. I come to know most surely what will result from my drinking eight double whiskies – that I shall be unable to drive my car safely, by having done such an action often before. I know the effect less surely by having seen the effect of others doing the action, or by having seen the effects of the result of the action when this was brought about unintentionally, all in similar circumstances to those in which I am considering doing the action; or by others telling me what happened on different occasions when they drank eight double whiskies. I know that this will lead to inability to drive less surely, because I suspect that I am different from the others (have more will-power, am more conscious of the dangers, am a better driver than the others anyway).

Less sure knowledge still is obtained by observing the result occur in somewhat different circumstances (e.g. when drinkers drink the whiskies much more quickly, or when tired). Still less sure knowledge is obtained by having observed goings-on only somewhat similar, and having to make allowance for the difference – e.g. I may only have seen the effects of men drinking different quantities of beer or gin. Or my knowledge may depend on reports given by others; then it will be still less certain. The witnesses may have exaggerated, not noticed differences in circumstances, etc.

The least certain knowledge of all is that which is reached by a process of more complicated inference from goings-on only remotely similar to A. However, it is difficult to see how a theory which predicted the occurrence of such evils as pain or death could have any justification unless the data on which the theory was built were cases of pain and death. If you had no knowledge of anything causing pain, how could other kinds of data substantiate predictions about pain? For pain is so different from other kinds of goings-on and has no natural connection with particular brain or nerve conditions rather than with others. (There is no reason for supposing that stimulation of this nerve will cause pain and of that one will cause pleasure, other than knowledge that that is what has happened in the past.)

So proximity to experience gives more certain knowledge. It is notorious that people are much more inclined to take precautions against disaster if they have suffered before themselves or if a similar disaster has happened to those close to them than if they are warned of the need for precaution by some impersonal distant authority. A man is far more inclined to take precautions against fire or burglary if he or his neighbours have suffered than if the police warn him that these things have happened in the next village. My point is that this is not just irrational perversity. It is the height of rationality to be influenced more by what is known better. People know better that it can happen to them if they know that it has happened to them or to others like them. With a mere police warning, they always have some reason for suspecting that police exaggerate or that things are different in the next village. What is irrational is not being influenced at all by the police warning; what is not irrational is being influenced more by goings-on closer at hand of which we have more intimate experience.

It follows from all this that we can only come to know that certain of our actions will have harmful consequences through prior experience (in some degree) of such harmful consequences. I come to know that drinking alcohol will give me a hangover most surely by having had it happen to me before, less surely by my having seen it happen to others before, less surely by others telling me that it has happened to them before, and least surely still by its being a remote prediction of some complex scientific theory. With the case of the worst evils it is not possible that my knowledge should be based on experience of what has happened to *me* before. I cannot know by experience that taking more and more heroin over a long period will cause death by having had it happen to me before. In such cases the most sure knowledge will be given by seeing it happen to many friends; less sure knowledge by seeing it happen on television (as in the British television documentary 'Gale is Dead'); still less sure knowledge by reading in a book that this happened before. Loss of limbs too is a consequence about which I can learn only by seeing or hearing of the experiences of others. But here too actually seeing a friend have to have his arm amputated as a result of standing too close to a dangerous machine in a factory and getting his arm trapped in it is rightly going to deter me from standing too close to the machine much better than is a notice which says 'Dangerous' (for the former gives me surer knowledge of the probable consequence of my action). It follows generally that my actions or negligence can only to my knowledge have really bad consequences if others have suffered such really bad consequences before. Among such really bad consequences are prolonged incurable suffering or death. These can only be among the evils which I can knowingly inflict on others, or through my negligence allow others to suffer, if others have suffered before.

. . .

There must be naturally occurring evils (i.e. evils not deliberately caused by men) if men are to know how to cause evils themselves or are to prevent evil occurring. And there have to be *many* such evils, if men are to have sure knowledge, for as we saw, sure knowledge of what will happen in future comes only by induction from many past instances. A solitary instance of a man dying after taking cyanide will not give to others very sure knowledge that in general cyanide causes death – may be the death on the occasion studied had a different cause, and the cyanide poisoning had nothing to do with it. And unless men have been bringing about evils of a certain kind deliberately recently, there have to be many recent naturally occurring evils if men are currently to have sure knowledge of how to bring about or prevent such evils.

. . .

Or suppose that men are to have the choice of building cities along earthquake belts, and so risking the destruction of whole cities and their populations hundreds of years later, or of avoiding doing so. How can such a choice be available to them unless they know where earthquakes are likely to occur and what their probable consequences are? And how are they to come to know this, unless earthquakes have happened due to natural and unpredicted causes, like the Lisbon Earthquake of 1755?

David Basinger, *Divine Power in Process Theism: A Philosophical Critique*, New York, State University of New York Press, 1988, pp. 56–60, 63–5

A God who is perfect in power, it is argued, could prevent all evil, and a God who is perfectly good would prevent all unnecessary evil. But there is undeniably a great deal of unnecessary evil – for example, there is a great deal of unnecessary human pain and suffering. Hence, something must give. The theist must either forfeit her belief in divine omnipotence, divine guidance or both.

It is not difficult to anticipate how most process theists respond. They acknowledge that we do experience a great deal of unnecessary evil. And they adamantly contend that God is perfectly good in the sense that God is doing all that can be done to eradicate such evil. But they deny that to affirm God's omnipotence is to affirm that God could eradicate all evil. God is omnipotent in the sense that God has all the power that it is logically possible for a being to possess. But all actual entities always possess some degree of self-determination. Thus, it is impossible for any entity – including God – to control unilaterally any state of affairs. God, of course, deplores all the unnecessary evil we experience and is always attempting to persuade the rest of reality to help co-create the best possible situation. But since God alone can insure nothing, the fact that evil states of affairs eventuate (and sometimes even proliferate) does not count against either God's power or goodness. [*Process theology speaks of a finite, limited, changing God who is not wholly in control of his creation, rather than an unlimited Creator.*]

Why exactly is this theodicy believed by process theists to be vastly superior to those affirmed by classical theists? The answer, as we have already implicitly seen, is based on the amount of power the God of classical theism allegedly possesses. As has been mentioned previously, not all classical theists believe that God always unilaterally controls all states of affairs. In fact some believe that God seldom does so. However, all classical theists do agree that God could unilaterally control all earthly affairs.

But if this is the case, most process theists argue, why does God not do more? Why do we not see fewer children dying of painful diseases? Why do we not see fewer people locked in psychological torment? The only responses available to the classical theist, we are told, are that what we experience is not really unnecessary evil (we just mistakenly perceive it as such) or that God is willing to tolerate unnecessary evil. But the former is implausible and the latter impugns God's moral integrity. Only by positing a God who cannot unilaterally intervene can the problem of evil be truly solved. For only then can we both admit the reality of unnecessary evil and justifiably maintain that God is good.

Is this assessment accurate? Does process thought offer the theist the most plausible theodicy? I am not totally convinced. It must be granted that the process critique of classical theodicies is based on an intuitively appealing moral concept. A perfectly good being who *could* unilaterally control all earthly affairs *would* eradicate all unnecessary evil. But it is not clear that the process application of this principle to classical thought is always consistent or fair.

First, is it true, as process theists contend, that the God of classical theism could unilaterally remove all evil? In one sense it is. All classical theists do believe that God has the power to control unilaterally all earthly affairs, including all evil states of affairs. But the nature and extent of such power (control) differ radically within the classical camp. And this is something that some process theists do not always appear to recognize clearly (or at least acknowledge).

Let us take, for example, David Griffins's initial critique of classical theodicies in his book *God, Power and Evil: A Process Theodicy*. Classical theists, we are told, affirm 'I' omnipotence, the belief 'that an omnipotent being can unilaterally affect any state of affairs, if that state of affairs is intrinsically possible.' (Such power, it must be understood, is not simply the power to control what humans do. It is the power to control what humans freely do, since any actual human option is an intrinsically possible state of affairs. It is the power, for example, to control unilaterally what a Hitler *freely* does.) Thus, Griffin continues, classical theists must view all evil as only apparent (nongenuine). For if God can unilaterally control everything (including our free choices), then, of course, any evil which remains must be desired by God as a necessary component in the best of all possible worlds.

...

But the majority of philosophical theists in the classical mode do not view things in this way. They do maintain that God is in total control of all states of affairs in the sense that God initially created *ex nihilo* the world system out of which all states of affairs are generated and has the power to manipulate unilaterally any person or thing at any time. But they emphatically deny that this entails that God has 'I' omnipotence –

that is, that God can unilaterally bring about any logically possible state of affairs.

. . .

God cannot unilaterally bring it about that we freely choose to perform good or evil activities. He can take away our freedom whenever this appears desirable and in this way unilaterally control us. But, if God has chosen to give us freedom, then God cannot unilaterally control the result. Much unnecessary, undeserved evil may in fact result.

Moreover, classical free will theists such as Plantinga believe that a world containing meaningful freedom and on balance more good than evil is a better world than one which contains neither. Thus, they hold that God is justified in allowing the unnecessary evil we experience even though God has the 'strength' to remove it. For to remove it would violate God's moral mandate to create the best *type* of world.

. . .

But what of natural evil, process theists will respond. It is one thing to contend that God's respect for human freedom prohibits God from continually vetoing even those free choices which result in significant evil; it is something quite different to contend that such respect prohibits God from intervening more frequently in the natural environment. For it is surely reasonable to maintain that God could cure a small child of cancer or calm a very destructive storm without significantly affecting the integrity of human freedom or significantly lessening the amount of good which exists.

In other words, even if process theists can be convinced that classical free will theists have a somewhat plausible response to the problem of *moral* evil, most process theists will continue to deny that free will theism can offer a plausible response to the problem of *natural* evil. For only a God who cannot unilaterally intervene in the natural order, they will adamantly maintain, can furnish the basis for an adequate natural theodicy.

This is, admittedly, the process theist's strongest challenge. But . . . classical free will theism is not without a response. The key to the process challenge in question is the assumption that there is little direct correlation between human freedom and the natural order. However, free will theists deny that this is the case. F. R. Tennant has argued, for example, that

> . . . it cannot be too strongly insisted that a world which is to be a moral order must be a physical order characterized by law or regularity. . . . The theist is only concerned to invoke the fact that the

law-abidingness . . . is an essential condition of the world being a theatre of moral life. Without such regularity in physical phenomena there could be no probability to guide us: no prediction, no prudence, no accumulation of ordered experience, no pursuit of premeditated ends, no formation of habit, no possibility of character or of culture. Our intellectual faculties could not have developed. . . . And without rationality, morality is impossible. (*Philosophical Theology*, Cambridge, Cambridge University Press, 1930, pp. 199–200)

In other words, classical free will theists maintain that every possible world containing free moral agents must be a world characterized by regularity.

However, if this is so, they continue, it appears that God cannot unilaterally bring it about that all events in nature are perfectly correlated with the needs of specific humans – that is, it seems that God cannot unilaterally remove all natural evil. For it seems that to achieve such a correlation would require a myriad of special interventions in nature, and this would conflict with the necessity for regularity. Or, to state this important point differently, free will theists believe that if God's intention was to create free, moral creatures, and morality requires regularity, then there is a definite sense in which God's ability to control nature – including those natural occurrences which generate unnecessary pain and suffering – is necessarily limited.

4.4 The cost-effectiveness of evil and the quantifying of pain

Stephen T. Davis, *Logic and the Nature of God*, London, Macmillan, 1983, pp. 110–11

At first glance, the FWD [*Free Will Defence*] seems less embarrassed than other theodicies by the amount of evil that exists in the world: the free will defender will simply say of all evil events that they are due not to God (or at least not directly to God) but rather to created free moral agents who choose to do evil. But at a deeper level, the FWD still seems open to this objection. For when we consider people like Hitler and events like the Holocaust we are bound to wonder whether the facility of free moral choice, which the FWD says God gave human beings, has turned out to be worth the price.

. . .

There are two points I wish to make about this. First, we do not know whether freedom is cost-effective. Let us be clear what it is we are evaluating: it is the policy decision God made (according to the FWD) to allow human beings moral freedom, i.e. freedom to do right or wrong without interference. Obviously, a correct decision on whether or not a given policy is cost-effective cannot be made till the results of the policy are in and can be evaluated. But how can we now correctly decide whether freedom will turn out to be cost-effective if we have no idea how human history will turn out? Perhaps it is true, as Christians believe, that the eschaton [*the 'Last Thing'*] holds in store for us such great goods that all pre-eschaton evils will be outweighed. We do not know whether this claim is true, and so we do not know whether God's policy will turn out to be cost-effective.

. . .

The second point is that only God knows whether freedom will turn out to be cost-effective. Only he knows how human history turns out, what our destiny is. Furthermore, only God is in a position to weigh huge goods and evils against each other in order to make correct judgements about whether, say, the Second World War was, on balance, a morally good or morally evil event. Thus only God is in a position to judge whether moral freedom will turn out to be worth the price.

David Brown, 'The Problem of Pain', in Robert Morgan (ed.), *The Religion of the Incarnation: Anglican Essays in Commemoration of Lux Mundi*, Bristol, Bristol Classical Press, 1989, pp. 49–53

For [Swinburne] the issue is not merely a logical one; it is also a question of probabilities. Can the fact of evil be accommodated within his cumulative, probabilistic case for theism? This is why he is concerned both with the quantities of evil in the world and with specific cases, and not just with the purely logical point with which he begins. It is thus this that leads him to say in respect of the amount of evil in the world: 'There must be naturally occurring evils . . . if men are to know how to cause evils themselves or are to prevent evil occurring. And there have to be *many* such evils (his emphasis), if men are to have sure knowledge, for as we saw, sure knowledge of what will happen in future comes only by induction from many past instances.' Again, as an illustration of his willingness to consider specific instances we might take the following: 'Actually seeing a friend have to have his arm amputated as a result of standing too close to a dangerous machine in a factory and getting his arm trapped in it is rightly going to deter me from standing too close to the machine much better than is a notice which says "Dangerous".'

...

[I]t does seem to me that Swinburne, admittedly in common with many others, has made a serious error of judgement in going beyond the purely logical problem into considerations of quantity and specific cases.

Taking quantity first, consider one of Newman's more controversial utterances: 'The Church holds that it were better for sun and moon to drop from heaven, for the earth to fail, and for all the millions who are upon it to die of starvation in extremest agony . . . than that one soul . . . should commit one single venial sin, should tell one wilful untruth though it harmed no one, or steal one poor farthing without excuse.' My point in quoting this particular utterance is not to endorse it, but simply to draw attention to how far removed traditional Christian morality is from any utilitarian calculus, any attempt to weigh good and evil in the same balance. Yet very often responses to the problem are phrased in ways which, whatever the intention, can easily admit of a utilitarian reading. For example, Davis in discussing the amount of evil in the world sees the issue in terms of whether 'this freedom has turned out to be cost-effective', whether we have 'the best possible balance of good over evil'. Likewise Swinburne responds to the objection that 'the game . . . is not worth the candle' by an admission that seems to concede that such weighing is the heart of the problem: 'This is, I believe, the crux of the problem of evil. It is not the fact of evil or the kinds of evil which are the real threat to theism; it is the quantity of evil.' It is little wonder therefore that, when theists themselves speak like this, their opponents also inevitably express the issue in terms of whether the good outweighs the evil it involves.

But, if we take this hint from Newman, what we shall see at stake is not at all the quantity of evils in the world but a different system of values. That is, the existence of evil in the world should simply be seen as a tragic consequence of certain goods being valued by God, not something that has to be weighed in the same balance as them. As Christians we attach supreme worth not to the creation of happiness, nor any attempt to balance out good and evil, but find it instead in the radical freedom that God has given us to shape our own destinies, including a type of character and virtues that simply would have no intelligibility, no meaning in the absence of pain. Thus it is just not the case that the argument with the non-believer takes place within a shared system of moral values. Rather, the heart of the debate lies in the fact that the Christian has opted for a different moral universe, one in which freedom, compassion, sympathy, courage and so forth exist. This is not to say that non-Christians never attach a similar high worth to these values; only to draw attention to the extent to which Christian as well as non-Christian can be infected in the modern world by utilitarian assumptions in making the issue of quantity primary.

But to this it may be objected that I have ignored one vital fact, that God can foresee the future and so must have had the choice between various possible worlds, some of which had more evil than the present one, some less, and so, even if he was not concerned with weighing evil against good, he still had the option of creating a world with less evil in it than at present and so quantity of evil remains a relevant issue, even if we are only comparing it with other possible levels of evil rather than with the good *per se*. Some contemporary philosophers would argue that, since God can only know what it is logically possible to know, he cannot know future, free human action since this remains undetermined until the individual makes his decision. That would be one way of responding, but even if we take the traditional account of omniscience it still remains unclear to me how we can make any objective assessment of the quantities of evil in the world. It is a commonplace in modern theology to speak of the need for a post-Auschwitz theology and indeed it is also a theme in contemporary philosophy, but I quite fail to see the point. God infinitely values each one of us and the tragic dimension of suffering would seem to me just as acute, whether we were to envisage just one individual suffering or millions. Here C. S. Lewis (1957, pp. 103–4) is more astute than many a modern writer: 'We must never make the problem of pain worse than it is by vague talk about the "unimaginable sum of human misery" . . . Search all time and space and you will not find that composite pain in anyone's consciousness. There is no such thing as a sum of suffering, for no one suffers it. When you have reached the maximum that a single person can suffer, we have, no doubt, reached something very horrible, but we have reached all the suffering there ever can be in the universe. The addition of a million fellow-sufferers adds no more pain.'

Since questions of quantity can enter consideration of the problem of evil in a number of different ways, it is perhaps worth pausing at this point to clarify what it is that is being affirmed and denied within the Christian tradition, as reflected in the writings of Newman and Lewis. As I understand it, the relevance of quantity is being denied in two specific ways. First, in contrast to those who think the argument is just about arithmetic, about what the total balance of pleasure and pain is, the claim is that the disagreement is in fact much more fundamental, there being no shared calculus in which to measure quantities, no sufficiently shared system of values. Secondly, given the traditional Christian stress on the unique, irreplaceable worth of each individual, the claim is that total quantity of pain in the world cannot be the issue, since that would be to suggest that persons were somehow dispensable in relation to a larger whole. Rather, the key issue must be the maximum amount of pain suffered by any particular individual. Of course, in a sense there is more tragedy in more suffering simply because more are suffering but the tragedy lies in what each suffers, not in some mysterious total summation of suffering. That being so, the only proper question of quantity must be whether God was justified in allowing the maximum quantity of suffering that can happen to the human condition to befall some particular individuals among us. There is thus no global question of quantity, only the tragic conflict between the moral value of freedom and the virtues and the maximum pain that any of these particular persons of infinite value could suffer.

Should someone still object that I have ignored one issue which remains crucial for them, namely that too many suffer this individual maximum of pain, my response would be that, once one has conceded that it is legitimate for God to let that happen to one individual, no further moral question can arise about the legitimacy of letting it happen to more than one. That one was already of infinite value in God's eyes, and so the tragic dimension in the divine decision is already present and in no way significantly increased by many others also suffering in this way. This is not to say that God would not try to keep the number who suffer to a minimum. But it is to claim that with free will there is no way of effectively controlling this and that the really important moral issue must be expressed in terms of the legitimacy of allowing just one individual to suffer, not by means of an irrelevant introduction of numbers.

The reference to Auschwitz may also be used to illustrate the other main failing in contemporary philosophical approaches, the appeal to specific cases. Part of the problem is that discussion of whether pain could serve some point in a particular case can easily lend credence to the idea that what is at stake is whether or not that particular pain was engineered by God to serve that point. In other words, by discussing particular cases it is very easy for a major shift of perspective to occur without its full implications being realised. For from the fact that God allows pain to occur as part of the general divine purposes, it by no means follows that such pain befalls this particular individual also as part of God's plan. The system is such that it is inevitable that some individual will suffer, but this does not mean that God has deliberately chosen a world in which it is this specifiable individual. Rather, it is entirely arbitrary whether the pain befalls A or B. That is to say, if the goods that God wants are to be realised, then tragically pain has to be part of the world, but who bears that pain is irrelevant. For the same results can be achieved, whoever it is. It is thus a logical mistake to discuss specific instances, because the philosophical 'solution' requires only that some individuals suffer, not that any actually uniquely identifiable individual should do so.

The main reason why this conclusion is resisted is, I think, because of the desire of philosopher as much as theologian for a total explanation. He thinks that there must be a reason why one individual suffers rather than another, and so wants to give that reason. Again, equally he may feel that it is incompatible with omnipotence to admit that any evil could finally frustrate the divine purpose and so all evil must ultimately be caught up to serve the good. Thus, for example, Nelson Pike tells that omnipotence can only be safeguarded if God succeeds in shaping all the evil that exists to ultimate divine purposes, while, to give a theological example, Barth expresses himself in very similar terms with his emphatic declaration that God 'would not be God if he were . . . restricted in his actions' and so he has no hesitation in concluding: 'The effect of the creature is in the hands of God. . . . It is wholly subordinated to the contexts of his wider purposes.'

That I just cannot believe. If God has given free will to man, this must have introduced a radical indeterminacy to the world, which even God cannot fully control. So if one accepts the free will defence there just is no avoiding the admission that there is an incurably tragic dimension to the creation . . .

Topics for discussion

1. To what extent is the problem of evil only a problem for the believer? Are perceptions of the amount of evil in the world increased or decreased by religious belief?
2. What moral assumptions lie behind the continuing modern use of Leibniz' phrase 'the best of all possible worlds', e.g. in Mackie? Is the Christian necessarily committed to such a utilitarian calculus?
3. To what extent is it in any case possible to quantify the total of good and evil in the world? Can we know the total (cf. Davis) or does it even make sense to use this as a criterion (cf. Schlesinger)?
4. Why does Swinburne think that 'many evils' are necessary for the growth of human knowledge? What problems, if any, do you detect in his argument?

5 Assuming that the notion of 'best possible' makes sense, would God then be under a moral obligation to create the best possible world? Does the doctrine of grace make a difference?
6 To what extent do Christian and non-Christian share the same moral view? May a difference in moral perspective be used to argue against the issue of quantity being a key issue?
7 Has process theology a more adequate response to the problem of evil than traditional approaches? Is Basinger right to concede that its strongest card is in respect of natural evil?

Acknowledgements

To SCM-Canterbury Press Ltd for a quotation from: *A Short Course in the Philosophy of Religion* by George Pattison; Penguin Books Ltd for a quotation from *The Brothers Karamazov* by Fyodor Dostoyevsky, translated by David Magarshack (Penguin Classics, 1958) copyright © David Magarshack, 1958; Blackwell Publishers Ltd for a quotation from *Theology and the Problem of Evil* by Kenneth Surin; Sheil Land Associates Ltd for a quotation from *Night* by Elie Wiesel copyright © Les Editions de Minuit 1958; HarperCollins Publishers Inc for quotations from *The Crucified God: The Cross of Christ as the Foundation and Criticism of Christian Theology* by Jürgen Moltmann, English translation copyright © 1974 by SCM Press Ltd; Oxford University Press for quotations from 'Jürgen Moltmann, the Jewish People and the Holocaust' by A. Roy Eckardt in *Journal of the American Academy of Religion* XLIV (4), 1976, *The Miracle of Theism: Arguments for and against the existence of God* by J.L. Mackie © John Mackie 1982, 'Suffering and Evil' by George N. Schlesinger in *Contemporary Philosophy of Religion* edited by Steven M. Cahn and David Shatz copyright © 1982 by Oxford University Press Inc, *The Existence of God* by Richard Swinburne © Richard Swinburne 1979; Darton, Longman & Todd Ltd for quotations from *Suffering* by Dorothee Soelle, *God's World* by Jeff Astley, *Imagining Evil* by Brian Horne copyright 1996 by Darton, Longman & Todd Ltd; Church House Publishing for quotations from *We Believe in God* © 1991 The Archbishops' Council; Cambridge University Press for quotations from 'Jewish Faith and the Holocaust' by Dan Cohn-Sherbok in *Religious Studies* 26(2), 1990, *Problems of Suffering in the Religions of the World* by John Bowker 1970, 'Divine Goodness and the Problem of Evil' by Terence Penelhum in *Religions Studies* 2, 1966–7, 'Self and Suffering: Deconstruction and Reflexive Definition in Buddhism and Christianity' by Philip A. Mellor in *Religious Studies* 27(1), 1991; Georges Borchardt Inc for a quotation from 'The 614th Commandment' in *The Jewish Return into History: Reflections in the Age of Auschwitz and a New Jerusalem* by Emil L. Fackenheim copyright © 1978 by Emil L. Fackenheim;

Pergamon Press for a quotation from '"Faith, Ethics and the Holocaust": Some Personal, Theological and Religious Responses to the Holocaust' by Immanuel Jakobovits in *Holocaust and Genocide Studies* 3(4) 1988; Crossroads, New York for a quotation from 'Salient Christian–Jewish Issues of Today' by A. Roy Eckardt in *Jews and Christians: Exploring the Past, Present and Future* edited by J.H. Charlesworth; T & T Clark for a quotation from 'Facing the Jews: Christian Theology after Auschwitz' by Johann-Baptist Metz in *Concilium* 175, 1984; Oxford University Press for a quotation from *Buddhism: Its Essence and Development* edited by E. Conze © Oxford University Press 1974; Random House Group Ltd for a quotation from *The Buddhist Handbook: A Complete Guide to Buddhist Teaching, Practice, History and Schools* by John Snelling published by Hutchinson; The Fellowship of Reconciliation for a quotation from *Vietnam: The Lotus in the Sea of Fire* by Thich Nhat Hanh; Princeton University Press for quotations from *Eighteen Upbuilding Discourses* by Søren Kierkegaard copyright © 1990 by Princeton University Press; James Clarke & Co Ltd for a quotation from *Gospel of Suffering* by Søren Kierkegaard; David Webster for 'Some explanatory notes on Buddhism'; Oxford University Press for a quotation from *Religion and Human Nature* by Keith Ward © Oxford University Press 1998; John Hick for a quotation from *Evil & the God of Love*; Routledge for a quotation from *The Problem of Evil* by M.B. Ahern; Cornell University for quotations from 'Must God Create the Best?' by Robert Merrihew Adams in *Philosophical Review* 81(3), 1972 copyright Cornell University; quotation from D. Basinger reprinted by permission from *Divine Power in Process Theism* edited by James R. Lewis, the State University of New York Press. © 1988 State University of New York. All rights reserved; Macmillan Publishers Ltd for a quotation from *Logic and the Nature of God* by Stephen T. Davis; and Gerald Duckworth & Co Ltd for a quotation from 'The Problem of Pain' by David Brown in *The Religion of the Incarnation: Anglican Essays in Commemoration of* Lux Mundi edited by Robert Morgan (Bristol Classical Press).

Further reading

Introductory and general

Astley, J. (2000) *God's World*, London, Darton, Longman & Todd, Chs 6 and 7.
Baker, J. A. (1970) *The Foolishness of God*, London, Collins, Chs 3–6.
Cowburn, J. (1979) *Shadows and the Dark: The Problems of Suffering and Evil*, London, SCM.
Davies, B. (1985) *Thinking about God*, London, Chapman, Ch. 8.
Davies, B. (1993) *An Introduction to the Philosophy of Religion*, Oxford, Oxford University Press, Ch. 3.
Davis, S. T. (ed.) (1981) *Encountering Evil: Live Options in Theodicy*, Edinburgh, T & T Clark.
Hebblethwaite, B. (1976) *Evil, Suffering and Religion*, London, Sheldon.
Hick, J. H. (1983, 1990) *Philosophy of Religion*, Englewood Cliffs, NJ, Prentice Hall, Ch. 4
Horne, B. (1996) *Imagining Evil*, London, Darton, Longman & Todd.
Lewis, C. S. (1957) *The Problem of Pain*, London, Collins.
Peterson, M., Hasker, W., Reichenbach, B. and Basinger, D. (1991) *Reason and Religious Belief*, New York, Oxford University Press, Ch. 6.
Peterson, M. L. (1997) 'The Problem of Evil', in P. L. Quinn and C. Taliaferro (eds) *A Companion to Philosophy of Religion*, Oxford, Blackwell, Ch. 50.
Sarot, M. (1999) *Living a Good Life in Spite of Evil*, Frankfurt am Main, Peter Lang.
Stump, E. and Murray, M. J. (eds) (1999) *Philosophy of Religion: The Big Questions*, Oxford, Blackwell, Part three.
Vardy, P. (1992) *The Puzzle of Evil*, London, HarperCollins.

1 Evil, protest and response

Cohn-Sherbok, D. (1990) 'Jewish Faith and the Holocaust', *Religious Studies*, 26, 2, pp. 278–93.

Eckardt, A. R. (1990) 'Salient Christian-Jewish Issues of Today: A Christian Exploration', in J. H. Charlesworth (ed.) *Jews and Christians: Exploring the Past, Present, and Future*, New York, Crossroad, pp. 151–84.

Eckardt, R. (1976) 'Jürgen Moltmann, The Jewish People and the Holocaust', *Journal of the American Academy of Religion*, CLIV, 4, pp. 675–91.

Garrison, J. (1982) *The Darkness of God: Theology After Hiroshima*, London, SCM.

Haynes, S. R. (1994) 'Christian Holocaust Theology: A Critical Reassessment', *Journal of the American Academy of Religion*, LXII, 2, pp. 553–85.

Jakobovits, I. (1988) 'Some Personal, Theological and Religious Responses to the Holocaust', *Holocaust and Genocide Studies*, 3, 4, pp. 371–81.

Metz, J.-B. (1984) 'Facing the Jews: Christian Theology after Auschwitz', in E. S. Fiorenza and D. Tracy (eds) *The Holocaust as Interruption* (*Concilium*, 175) Edinburgh, T & T Clark, pp. 26–33.

Moltmann, J. (1974) *The Crucified God*, ET London, SCM, Ch. 6.

Ricoeur, P. (1985) 'Evil, A challenge to Philosophy and Theology', *Journal of the American Academy of Religion*, LIII, 3, pp. 635–48.

Sarot, M. (1991) 'Auschwitz, Morality and the Suffering of God', *Modern Theology*, 7, 2, pp. 135–52.

Sölle, D. (1975) *Suffering*, ET London, Darton, Longman & Todd.

Surin, K. (1986) *Theology and the Problem of Evil*, Oxford, Blackwell.

Sutherland, S. R. (1977) *Atheism and the Rejection of God*, Oxford, Blackwell.

Tilley, T. (1990) *The Evils of Theodicy*, Washington, DC, Georgetown University Press.

Wiesel, E. (1981) *Night*, ET London, Penguin.

2 The Buddha and Kierkegaard on suffering: Two religions compared

Bowker, J. (1970) *Problems of Suffering in the Religions of the World*, Cambridge, Cambridge University Press, Ch. 6.

Cupitt, D. (1992) *The Time Being*, London, SCM.

Kierkegaard, S. (1955) *Gospel of Sufferings*, ET Cambridge, James Clarke.

Kierkegaard, S. (1958) *Edifying Discourses: A Selection*, ed. P. L. Holmer, ET London, Collins, especially pp. 78–114. (Translation by D. F. and L. M. Swenson.)

Kierkegaard, S. (1990) *Eighteen Upbuilding Discourses*, ed. H. V. Hong and

E. H. Hong, ET Princeton, NJ, Princeton University Press, 1990, especially pp. 109–24 and 233–51. (Translation by H. V. and E. H. Hong.)

Mellor, P. A. (1991) 'Self and Suffering: Deconstruction and Reflexive Definition in Buddhism and Christianity', *Religious Studies*, 27, 1, pp. 49–63.

Pannikar, R. (1978) 'Sunyata and Pleroma: The Buddhist and Christian Response to the Human Predicament', in R. Pannikar, *The Intra-Religious Dialogue*, New York, Paulist, pp. 77–100.

General texts on Buddhism

Gethin, R. (1998) *The Foundations of Buddhism*, Oxford, Oxford University Press.

Harvey, P. (1990) *An Introduction to Buddhism: Teachings, History and Practices*. Cambridge, Cambridge University Press.

Harvey, P. (2001) *An Introduction to Buddhist Ethics*, Cambridge, Cambridge University Press.

Jackson, R. R. and Makransky, J. J. (eds) (2000) *Buddhist Theology: Critical Reflections by Contemporary Buddhist Scholars*, Richmond, Curzon.

Kalupahana, D. (1976) *Buddhist Philosophy: A Historical Analysis*, Hawaii, University Press of Hawaii.

Skilton, A. (1997) *A Concise History of Buddhism*, Windhorse Publications, Birmingham.

Williams, P. with Tribe, A. (2000) *Buddhist Thought: A Complete Introduction to the Indian Tradition*, London, Routledge.

General texts on Kierkegaard

Collins, J. (1954) *The Mind of Kierkegaard*, London, Secker & Warburg.
Gardiner, P. (1988) *Kierkegaard*, Oxford, Oxford University Press.
Pattison, G. (1997) *Kierkegaard and the Crisis of Faith*, London, SPCK.
Rose, T. (2001) *Kierkegaard's Christocentric Theology*, Aldershot, Ashgate.

3 The varieties of theodicy

Adams, M. M. and Adams, R. M. (eds) (1990) *The Problem of Evil*, Oxford, Oxford University Press.

Davis, S. T. (ed.) (1981) *Encountering Evil: Live Options in Theodicy*, Edinburgh, T & T Clark.

Farrer, A. (1962) *Love Almighty and Ills Unlimited*, London, Collins.
Geach, P. (1977) *Providence and Evil*, Cambridge, Cambridge University Press, Chs 4–7.
Hick, J. (1966, 1977, 1985) *Evil and the God of Love*, London, Macmillan.
Hick, J. (1973) *God and the Universe of Faiths*, London, Macmillan, Chs 4 and 5.
Hume, D. (1779) *Dialogues Concerning Natural Religion*, various editions, Parts X and XI.
Levenson, J. D. (1988) *Creation and the Persistence of Evil: The Jewish Drama of Divine Omnipotence*, Princeton, NJ, Princeton University Press.
Metz, J.-B. (1994) 'Suffering unto God', *Critical Inquiry*, 20, 4, pp. 611–22.
Midgley, M. (1984) *Wickedness: A Philosophical Essay*, London, Routledge & Kegan Paul.
Mitchell, B. (ed.) (1971) *The Philosophy of Religion*, Oxford, Oxford University Press, articles by Mackie and Plantinga, pp. 92–120.
Plantinga, A. (1975) *God, Freedom and Evil*, London, George Allen & Unwin, Part I.
Sams, K. M. (1994) *Escape from Paradise: Evil and Tragedy in Feminist Theology*, Minneapolis, MN, Fortress.
Schoonenberg, P. (1965) *Man and Sin: A Theological View*, ET London, Sheed and Ward.
Sponheim, P. R. (1984) 'Sin and Evil', in C. E. Braaten and R. W. Jenson (eds) *Christian Dogmatics*, 1, Philadelphia, Fortress, pp. 359–464.
Ward, K. (1998) *Religion and Human Nature*, Oxford, Oxford University Press, Ch. 8.
Ward, K. (1996) *Religion and Creation*, Oxford, Oxford University Press, Part III.
Westermann, C. (1971) *Creation*, ET London, SPCK, Ch. 4.
Williams, N. P. (1927) *The Ideas of the Fall and of Original Sin*, London, Longmans, Green.

4 The logic of theodicy

Adams, M. M. (1986) 'Redemptive Suffering', in R. Audi and W. G. Wainwright (eds) *Rationality, Religious Belief and Moral Commitment*, Ithaca, New York, Cornell University Press, pp. 248–67.
Adams, M. (1990) 'Horrendous Evils and the Goodness of God', in M. M. Adams and R. M. Adams (eds) *The Problem of Evil*, Oxford, Oxford University Press, pp. 209–21.
Adams, M. M. (1999) *Horrendous Evils and the Goodness of God*, Ithaca, NY, Cornell University Press.

Further reading

Adams, R. M., (1987) 'Must God Create the Best?', in R. M. Adams, *The Virtue of Faith*, New York, Oxford University Press, pp. 51–64.

Ahern, M. B. (1971) *The Problem of Evil*, London, Routledge & Kegan Paul.

Basinger, D. (1988) *Divine Power in Process Theism: A Philosophical Critique*, New York, State University of New York Press.

Brown, D. (1989) 'The Problem of Pain', in R. Morgan (ed.) *The Religion of the Incarnation*, Bristol, Bristol Classical Press, pp. 46–59.

Davis, S. T. (1983) *Logic and the Nature of God*, London, Macmillan, Ch. 7.

Griffin, D. (1976) *God, Power and Evil: A Process Theodicy*, Philadelphia, Pennsylvania, Westminster.

Mackie, J. L. (1982) *The Miracle of Theism*, Oxford, Oxford University Press, Ch. 9.

Penelhum, T. (1990) 'Divine Goodness and the Problem of Evil', in M. M. Adams and R. M. Adams (eds) *The Problem of Evil*, Oxford, Oxford University Press, pp. 69–82.

Schlesinger, G. N. (1982) 'Suffering and Evil', in S. M. Cahn and D. Shatz (eds) *Contemporary Philosophy of Religion*, New York, Oxford University Press, pp. 25–31.

Swinburne, R. (1979) *The Existence of God*, Oxford, Oxford University Press, Ch. 11.

Swinburne, R. (1998) *Providence and the Problem of Evil*, Oxford, Oxford University Press.

Index of subjects

absorbed / unabsorbed evil 81–2
  see also dysteleological suffering
Arahant / Arahat 33–4
arbitrariness of evil 20–1, 22–3, 77–8
atheism 15–17
Augustine / Augustinian theodicy 3,
  60–2, 64–9, 72–4
Auschwitz, see Holocaust

bad faith 11–13
baptism 66
best possible world 3, 79–84
blasphemy 9, 16
Buddha / Buddhism
  and suffering 1, 30–44, 50–4
  early Buddhism 2, 36, 52
  enlightenment in 31, 35
  experience in 40–1
  four noble truths of 30, 35, 53–4
  middle-way of 51
  noble eightfold path of 30, 32–3, 35, 54
  Theravada 52
burden, light 49–50

compassion 43–4
cost-effectiveness of evil 3, 93–4
Council of Trent 75
craving 2, 35–6, 53–4
cross / crucifixion 15–25

dereliction, cry of 17, 23
determinism / indeterminacy 69–71, 98
devil, the 15–16, 67
Dhammapada 31
Dostoevsky and suffering / evil 7–11,
  15
dukkha 30, 32, 35, 53–4
dysteleological suffering 77–8

endurance 25

eschatology 77
  see also heaven; paradise
evil, definition of 59
existentialism 8

Fall, the 61, 72–5
free will defence 3, 60–2, 69–75, 91–2,
  92–3, 98
FWD, see free will defence

harmony 6, 9
heaven 62
hell 15, 19, 62
Hitler 25–7
  see also Holocaust, the
Holocaust, the 1–2, 13, 14, 17–19, 25–9

indeterminacy, see determinism /
  indeterminacy; free will defence
infinite value 97
intervention, divine 75
Irenaeus / Irenaean theodicy 3, 60–2, 64,
  74

Jesus and suffering / evil 1, 2, 14–25
  see also cross / crucifixion
Jewish theodicy, see Holocaust
Job, Book of 2, 6–7, 47–9

Kierkegaard and suffering / evil 2, 7,
  46–50
knowledge 92–3
  of evil 87–90

Leibniz and suffering / evil 6, 79–84
libertarianism 69
  see also free will defence
Lisbon earthquake 5, 80
logical problem of evil 2, 56, 58
  see also 79–98

Index of subjects

Manicheism 65
maximizing satisfaction 84–7
Moltmann and suffering / evil 14–19, 29
moral blindness 13
moral evil 1, 60–2, 91–2
  see also Fall, the; sin; free will defence
moral imagination 13

natural evil 1, 59, 60–2, 87–90, 92–3
  see also vale of soul-making
Nazis 26
  see also Holocaust
Nirvana 41–3
  see also Buddha / Buddhism and suffering
Noah 64
non-being, evil as 61, 64–9

omnipotence 2, 56, 58, 90–4, 98
omniscience 2, 56, 58
original guilt 74–5
outrage 1, 5–6
  see also protest theodicy / atheism

paradise 25–6
  hedonistic 75
Paul and suffering / evil 6
physical evil 1, 59
  see also natural evil
Plato 83–4
plenitude, principle of 3, 61, 62–4
power 28, 90–4
  see also omnipotence
predestination 70
process theology / theodicy 90–4
Prometheus 9, 16
protest theodicy / atheism 5–29

quantifying suffering / evil 3, 94–8
questions, unprofitable 35–6, 37–40, 52

rebellion 10, 16–17, 68
resurrection 24

Satan 16, 67–8
  see also devil, the
Sartre and suffering / evil 8, 11–12
screening of God 63–4
second-order goods / evils 81
self, the 44–6
self-sacrifice 43–4
  see also cross / crucifixion
Shoah, the, *see* Holocaust, the
sin 54, 58–9
  original sin 3, 72–5
  see also moral evil
swastika 18
Swinburne and suffering / evil 12–13

theodicy 1, 57
Theopaschite controversy 23
Tipitakas 30–4
transworld depravity 72
Trinity 23–4
truths, concerned 46–7

unavenged suffering 10–11
unsatisfactoriness 2
  see also dukkha

vale of soul-making 3, 60, 75–8, 80–2
Voltaire and suffering / evil 5–6

weighing evil, *see* quantifying evil

Index of names

Adams, M. M. 1, 105–6
Adams, R. M. 1, 82–4, 105–7
Ahern, M. B. 79–80, 107
Allen, D. 1
Aquinas, St Thomas 60
Astley, J. 59–62, 103
Audi, R. 106
Augustine (of Hippo) 3, 60, 62, 64–9, 72, 74

Baker, J. A. 103
Barth, K. 98
Barton, J. 19–21
Basinger, D. 78, 90–3, 103, 107
Bowker, J. 41–3, 104
Braaten, C. E. 106
Brown, D. 2, 20–1, 94–8, 107
Brown, S. C. 13
Buddha 30–5
Burnaby, J. 67
Burtt, E. A. 37–40

Cahn, S. M. 84–7, 107
Cain 16
Calvin, J. 60
Camus, A 16
Cohn-Sherbok, D. 25–6, 103
Collins, J. 105
Conrad, J. 12
Conze, E. 30
Council of Trent 75
Cowburn, J. 103
Cupitt, D. 104
Charlesworth, J. H. 28, 104

Davids, R. 43
Davies, B. 2, 103
Davis, S. T. 80, 93–5, 98, 103, 105, 107
Doctrine Commission of the General Synod of the Church of England 22–5

Dosto(y)evsky, F. 1, 7–11, 15–16

Eckardt, A. L. 28
Eckardt, A. R. 1–2, 17–19, 28, 104

Fackenheim, E. L. 26–7
Farrer, A. 59, 62–4, 106
Fenelon, F. 45
Fiorenza, E. S. 29, 104
Flannery, E. H. 18–19
Flew, A. G. N. 69

Gardiner, P. 105
Garrison, J. 104
Gautama, Prince Siddhartha, *see* Buddha
Geach, P. 106
Gethin, R. 105
Glatzer, N. N. 2
Griffin, D. 91, 107

Hanh, T. N. 43–4
Harvey, P. 105
Hasker, W. 103
Haynes, S. R. 104
Hebblethwaite, B. 34–6, 103
Hick, J. H. 3, 60, 62, 69–70, 76–8, 103, 106
Hitler, A. 25–7
Holmer, P. L. 104
Hong, E. H. 46–9, 104–5
Hong, H. V. 46–9, 104–5
Horne, B. 2, 62, 64–9, 103
Hume, D. 76–7, 106

Irenaeus, St 3, 60, 74

Jackson, R. R. 105
Jakobovits, I. 27–8, 104
Jenson, R. W. 106
Jesus 1, 2, 14–15

Index of names

Kalupahana, D. 105
Kant, I. 5
Keats, J. 60
Kehl, M. 45
Kierkegaard, S. 2, 7, 46–50, 55, 104–5
King, M. L. 43–4

Levenson, J. D. 106
Leibniz 3, 6, 60, 79–80, 82–3, 98
Lewis, C. S. 96, 103

Mackie, J. L. 2, 56–7, 69, 80–2, 98, 106–7
MacKinnon, D. M. 1
Mahadevan, T. M. P. 30–4
Makransky, J. J. 105
Mellor, P. A. 2, 44–6, 105
Metz, J.-B. 29, 104, 106
Midgley, M. 106
Mitchell, B. 106
Moltmann, J. 1, 14, 17–19, 29, 104
Morgan, R. 20–1, 94–8, 107
Murray, M. J. 103

Newman, J. H. 95–6

Origen 67–8

Pannikar, R. 105
Pattison, G. 1, 5–8, 105
Paul, St 6
Penelhum, T. 2, 58–9, 107
Peterson, M. L. 103
Phillips, D. Z. 13
Pike, N. 98
Plantinga, A. 70–2, 78, 92, 106
Plato 83–4
Plotinus 65
Prometheus 9, 16

Quinn, P. L. 103

Reichenbach, B. 103
Ricoeur, P. 12, 104

Rose, T. 105

Sams, K. M. 106
Sarot, M. 103–4
Sartre, J.-P. 8, 11
Schiller, J. C. F. 15
Schleiermacher, F. D. E. 60
Schlesinger, G. N. 84–7, 98, 107
Schoonenberg, P. 106
Shatz, D. 84–7, 107
Skilton, A. 105
Snelling, J. 40–1
Socrates 20, 85–6
Sölle, D. 21–2, 29, 104
Sponheim, P. R. 106
Strindberg, J. A. 15
Stump, E. 103
Surin, K. 1, 11–13, 104
Sutherland, S. R. 104
Swenson, D. F. 104
Swenson, L. M. 104
Swinburne, R. 3, 12–13, 87–90, 94–5, 98, 107

Taliaferro, C. 103
Tennant, F. R. 60, 92
Terrien, S. 2
Thyagarajan, A. 30–4
Tilley, T. 104
Tracy, D. 29, 104
Tribe, A. 105

Vardy, P. 2–3, 103
Voltaire 3, 6
von Balthasar, H. U. 44–5

Wainwright, W. G. 106
Ward, K. 59, 72–6, 106
Webster, D. 50–4
Westermann, C. 106
Wiesel, E. 1, 14, 17, 104
Williams, N. P. 106
Williams, P. 105